Researching

Online

Researching Online

Third Edition

David Munger

Daniel Anderson
University of North Carolina

Bret Benjamin
University of Texas—Austin

Christopher Busiel
University of Texas—Austin

Bill Parades-Holt
University of Texas—Austin

LONGMAN

An imprint of Addison Wesley Longman, Inc.

New York • Reading, Massachusetts • Menlo Park, California • Harlow, England
Don Mills, Ontario • Sydney • Mexico City • Madrid • Amsterdam

Publishing Partner: Anne Smith
English Editor: Lynn Huddon
Supplements Editor: Donna Campion
Text Design: Digital Text Construction
Electronic Page Makeup: Dianne Hall

Researching Online, 3/e by David Munger, et al.

ISBN 0-321-05802-X

99000102—DM—9876543

Contents

Preface

The process of writing the third edition of *Researching Online* brings to mind a traditional story from Italy. A young tenor was performing a difficult aria in an opera house known for its demanding audiences. To his surprise, the audience's thunderous applause brought him back the stage for encore after encore. After his fifth performance, he told the audience that he appreciated their gratitude, but his voice was failing and he could sing no more. A disgruntled voice from the back of the hall retorted, "you're going to do it until you get it right!"

With *Researching Online,* we feel fortunate to have the opportunity to try to get it right once a year. Because the Internet changes so rapidly, a new edition each year—a rarity in the textbook industry—gives us a chance to update expired URLs, add new features, and adapt at a pace that *almost* approaches that of technology.

Researching Online shows students how to do research on the Internet in an easy-to-follow, step-by-step format. It's written in plain English, with clear examples of the types of materials students may encounter in their own research. The Internet is presented in the order that students will most likely encounter it: first, they learn how to get on-line. Then they learn about Internet resources like e-mail, the Web, and newsgroups. Finally, they get clear, easy to follow instructions on creating their own Web pages. This edition features a new chapter on managing Web research, and expanded chapters on copyright and documenting sources.

Everything about *Researching Online* has been designed to make it the most useful possible tool for anyone doing research on the Internet. Its compact size allows it to consume little desk space in crowded computer labs. Specialized vocabulary is **bold and underlined** to alert readers to terms defined in the glossary. Text users must input is displayed in a `special typeface` to make easy to recognize. URLs are displayed in **_bold italic_** and without confusing angle brackets. Most importantly, critical concepts are both explained in the text and reinforced visually with real-world examples.

Features in this edition

Netiquette Tips

"Netiquette Tips" throughout give practical advice about conduct on the Internet—such as when to use smilies in your e-mail. Located near the the Internet resources they describe, these boxes are formatted to stand out, giving special notice to the information they contain.

A new chapter on managing Web research

This new section is especially useful for students who must work in computer labs rather than on their own computer. It includes tips on saving files, printing Web pages, and using helper applications such as RealAudio.

A new chapter on copyright online

Copyright is defining the future of the Internet. This new chapter offers detailed advice about when and how to use copyrighted material.

An expanded chapter on documenting online sources

This chapter has been completely revised to describe documenting sources as a process. It now offers twice as many models and graphics that simplify the task of documenting sources.

Expanded coverage of evaluating online sources

This section now includes an annotated example, additional guidelines, and more focused coverage of the differences between online and traditional research sources.

A fully revised chapter on researching literature

This completely revised Chapter 11, A Case Study: Researching Literature on the Internet now approaches the topic from the perspective of a student completing the entire research process.

A new directory of URLs referenced in the text

This handy reference makes it easy for students to locate the resources mentioned in the text.

New guidelines for writing on the Web

These new guidelines offer students practical advice for creating more usable Web sites.

Updated examples throughouth the text

More realistic examples are now fully integrated into the text.

Acknowledgments

This book evolved out of the groundbreaking book *Teaching Online* by Daniel Anderson, Bret Benjamin, Christopher Busiel, and Bill Paredes-Holt. We remain indebted to Karen Milholland for much of the research behind the literature research chapter. Deanna Campbell provided additional insight and inspiration. Connie Wessner provided a great sounding board for the HTML chapter. Jimmy and Nora Munger continue to demonstrate how easy computers can be to use and learn from. Anne Smith and Lynn Huddon at Longman were rock-solid in their support of this book. Jennifer Ahrend provided brilliant copyediting. Donna Campion helped immeasurably in seeing it through to the finish. We'd like to express special thanks to the reviewers of this edition: Michelle R. Kendrick, Washington State University—Vancouver, Michele Guthrie Maynard, University of Texas, and Craig Branham, St. Louis University.

Chapter 1

Introduction to the Internet

It's 3:00 A.M., your paper on coral reefs is due in six hours, you need to know the scientific name of the crown of thorns starfish, and every library in your time zone is closed.

or

You're not sure about the reliability of a source you want to use in an oral presentation about the conflict in Kosovo, but it's too new to have published reviews.

or

You need to find every reference to *eyes* in *Macbeth*.

or

You'd like to collaborate on a political science project with your lab partner from last semester—but she's in Germany this term on a semester abroad.

The **Internet** can be part of the solution to each of these problems. For finding that one last source at 3:00 A.M., try a search engine on the **World Wide Web**. To verify the reliability of a source for which you can't find a published review, try posting a query on a **Usenet newsgroup**. To search for specific words or phrases in Shakespeare's plays, try the The Complete Plays of William Shakespeare, at *http://www.ke .com.au/cgi-bin/texhtml?form=Shake*. To collaborate with someone in another part of the world, communicate with **e-mail**, then work interactively using an **IRC** or a **MUD**.

Can the Internet answer all of your research questions? Well, it doesn't contain the entire archives of the Library of Congress or even every back issue of the *New York Times* (not yet, anyway). It can't perform original research experiments or help you communicate with someone who doesn't have

Internet access. And while it can help you reach people and resources on the other side of the world, it's certainly no substitute for live, one-on-one interaction with real people and real things.

The Internet is at its best when it helps make your research experience easier, more thorough, and more collaborative. At other times, you may need to rely on the permanence and authority of resources found in traditional libraries. This book will help guide you through the process of integrating online sources into your research.

Use the Internet to inform your research

The Internet can be thought of as an enormous, constantly evolving conversation in which users meet to discuss almost any imaginable topic. There are dozens of ways you can benefit from using the Internet; for instance, you can easily:

- Access online resources to support your research, including many resources like databases and live "cams" that aren't available in any other format.
- Communicate with authors of important sources or experts in various fields of study.
- Meet online with other researchers to discuss a common topic.
- Design and publish the results of your research on the World Wide Web, offering an interactive Web site, links to other Internet resources about the topic, video clips of major figures, and forums for conversation among users.

The Internet is a worldwide network of computers that are connected to each other in many different ways. Each of these different sorts of connections is useful for different kinds of work. The most important Internet services are listed below.

World Wide Web. Now the most important part of the Internet, the Web allows you to quickly and easily navigate through millions of **hypertext** sites containing images, text, sound, motion pictures, and even databases.

E-mail. E-mail allows you to quickly exchange messages and computer files with anyone connected to the Internet.

Usenet newsgroups. Newsgroups are a vast collection of specialized electronic bulletin boards where (usually) anyone can post or respond to a message.

Listservs. A specialized type of e-mail, listservs are moderated or unmoderated discussion groups on specified topics.

Telnet, FTP, and Gopher. Older parts of the Internet, these are ways of accessing files and programs on distant computers.

IRCs and MU*s. These are services which allow you to communicate with other users in real time.

Online versus printed sources

Plan when to use online sources and
when to use traditional sources in your research

Online sources and printed sources each have strengths and weaknesses. Deciding when to use which type of source isn't a matter of applying a simple formula. To determine what type of resource will be most valuable for your research project, you'll first need to consider how you are planning on using the source. Table 1.1 summarizes the most important differences between online and printed sources, but remember that there are many different types of printed and online sources—these guidelines don't necessarily apply to all cases.

Suppose you are researching endangered loggerhead sea turtles on the Florida coast. For authoritative information about the physiology and behavior of sea turtles, books and journal articles will probably offer the most reliable information. But the Internet is only place you'll find a real-time map of the movements of sea turtles as they are electronically tracked by researchers.

The Internet and print sources can offer different types of information, but they can also offer the same information. For example, you can find the text of thousands of classic works of literature such as Jane Austen's *Pride and Prejudice* on the World Wide Web, and you can also find many of the same works in your school library. How do you decide which source to use in your research? The answer depends on how you'll be using the information.

Select sources based on the demands of your project

Each project has different demands. A thesis paper on Jane Austen may require that you find the most authoritative edition of *Pride and Prejudice* available. A two-page outline for an in-class presentation on descriptions of dancing in *Pride and*

Online Resources	Printed Resources
Can be easily modified	Unchangeable except in a new edition
Can include many different media	Only include text and and images
May appear different to different users	Appear the same to each user
Allow input from users	Do not allow user input
Inexpensive to produce	Relatively expensive to produce
Allow almost anyone to publish information	Publishing closely monitored by "gatekeepers" such as editors and librarians
Generally not subjected to scholarly review	Often reviewed by scholars for accuracy and relevance

Table 1.1: Comparison of online resources and printed resources

Prejudice may require a searchable version of the text, such as those available online. Here is a list of issues to consider as you determine which sources will be most useful for your project.

1. **Timeliness**. In many cases, particularly with newsgroups and listservs, the Internet can provide more up-to-date information than traditional sources. And while daily newspapers offer a reliable, traditional research source, most major newspapers are now available on the World Wide Web, with searchable indexes of past issues.
2. **Authority**. Printed resources, especially those available in a college library, are often reviewed by scholars for accuracy and relevance—if this sort of authority is required for your project, refereed journals and academic books will probably be your most important sources. In other cases, an Internet source may carry more authority than the resources available in the library. For example, you may find a facsimile edition of a classic work of literature on the Web.

3. **Course requirements.** Your instructor may require that all (or a certain number) of your research sources be from academic books or refereed journal articles. In this case, though you may want to use an online service to locate resources, you will most likely find the actual resources in a library. On the other hand, if your instructor requires that you interview an expert in a field, you may be more likely to make that contact via the Internet.

4. **Accessibility.** If everyone had access to a library with thousands of journal subscriptions and millions of volumes, traditional sources might often be the best option. However, most of us don't have that luxury, so online sources become a more important component of the research process.

5. **Reliability.** Pay close attention to the matters discussed in the following section, "Evaluate all electronic sources you use." As you locate both printed and online sources in your research, evaluate them according to the criteria outlined below. When you have a choice, select the most reliable sources, whether online or in print.

Evaluate all electronic sources you use

One of the most important virtues of the Internet is its universality. For about a hundred dollars, anyone can register a World Wide Web address and have as much of a Web presence as Microsoft or IBM. The Internet has no gatekeeper (for that matter, it has no single, central gate).

While the universality of the Internet can be good in that it allows previously marginalized voices to be heard, it also adds a new layer of difficulty for researchers. The gatekeepers of traditional research sources—editors, academics, and librarians—have always made it a relative certainty that any source in a college library meets a basic standard of reliability and relevance. Since the Internet lacks those gatekeepers, you're just as likely to encounter uninformed drivel there as you are to find a unique resource that's unavailable in any other form.

Additionally, materials found online will often differ a great deal from those in print. Resources may feature graphics, sound, and video, for example. What's more, Internet sources may have a more (or less) impressive appearance than traditional "published" articles.

When you're evaluating an electronic source, above all, you must ask questions, and never assume the source is an authority. Here are some guidelines you can use to evaluate an electronic source:

- Who is the author?
- Is a link to the author's **home page** (see page 69) and/ or e-mail contact information provided?
- Does the author have an academic or professional affiliation?
- Who is the sponsor of the resource? An academic organization? A business?
- What are the potential biases/hidden agendas of the author and/or the sponsor of the resource?
- Is the resource regularly updated? Are the **links** provided up to date?
- Does the resource follow good principles of design and proper grammar and style? (Note: Good design is not necessarily "flashy." A simple, conservative site can be more tasteful than one bristling with graphics and sound effects.)
- Are the articles reviewed by peers? (Note: Beware of "Top 500 Web site" awards and the like—always check *them* out using the standards given here. There are even Web sites which are completely devoted to giving out phony awards—for a hilarious example, check out *http://www.thecorporation.com/icon/icon .html.*)

Writing instructors and librarians have recognized the difficulty in evaluating electronic sources, and some have attempted to generate uniform criteria for evaluating these sources. You may want to check out the Using Cybersources Web site at *http://www.devry-phx.edu/lrnresrc/dowsc /integrty.htm* for a detailed set of guidelines on how to evaluate a Web source, as well as links to other sites with more suggestions.

Figure 1.1 shows an example of a Web site that provides many answers to the above questions. The site is well designed, gives information about the author's credentials, and is regularly updated. Note that the ads and awards on the site don't necessarily add or remove from the site's value, but should be investigated in case they reveal a bias or hidden agenda. Before you use an electronic source in your research, make sure you find answers to the questions in this section.

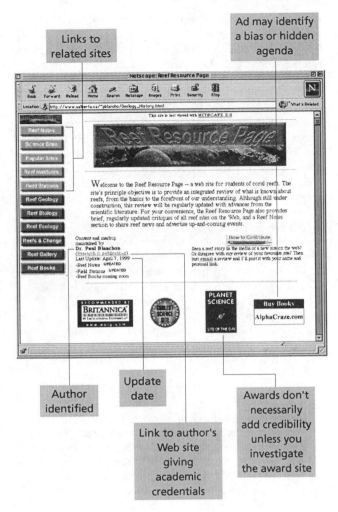

Figure 1.1: What to look for when evaluating a Web site

How the Internet works

The Internet is vast collection of computers that communicate with each other in a variety of ways. For the most part, you will be accessing information found on **servers**, Internet computers and computer programs equipped to provide information to anyone who knows how to ask.

For example, when you visit the Yahoo! Web site, you type the site's address in your Web **browser** (a program like

Netscape Navigator or Microsoft Internet Explorer). The information you request resides on a server in the California. The server sends your browser the information you need, often passing it through many other computers before it reaches you.

If you want to use the Internet to send an e-mail message to the president of the United States, you use an e-mail program (like Eudora or Navigator) on your computer to compose the message. The e-mail program sends the message to the White House server (again possibly with several intermediate steps). Then, the president (or more likely, a White House intern) uses another program on a computer to check for mail on the White House server, at which point the server sends the message to the president's computer, where he can use his e-mail software to read your message. You can try this out for yourself. The president's e-mail **address** (see Chapter 2) is *president@whitehouse.gov.*

Other Internet software, such as e-mail programs like Pine and browser programs like Lynx, actually reside on servers, allowing users to read mail and browse the World Wide Web using only a terminal. For the most part, this book assumes you are accessing the Internet using software that resides on your own computer, which we recommend because it is the easiest and most convenient to use.

Connecting to the Internet

Connecting via the campus network. Most colleges and universities have a network of computers that is connected to the Internet. In many cases, computers are available for student use in computer labs, the library, or in dorms. The software you need to access the Internet has been installed on the computers; all you need to do is learn to use the software on those computers, and you're in business (see Chapters 2–7). For e-mail, you'll need to establish an e-mail account—usually handled through your campus computer services department.

Connecting using your own computer. If you have your own computer, getting connected to the Internet is a little more complicated—but once you're connected, it's a lot more convenient than relying on public computers. If you have a brand-new computer, it's very likely that all the software you need is already installed on your computer. If you have inherited an older computer, especially one that has never been connected to the Internet, you may have to do a bit of scrambling to obtain the client software you need.

At the bare minimum, you need a connection program (usually a PPP program and a TCP/IP program), a **mailreader**, and a **Web browser**. An easy way to get all this software is to upgrade your computer to the newest operating system—either Windows or Mac—which will include Internet connectivity software. If you need to subscribe to an Internet service provider for dial-up access (see below), the software is often provided as part of your subscription cost. Or just visit a computer store—there you can often find free copies of the latest Internet software, ready to install.

Direct Access. Many institutions offer direct access to the Internet in campus dorms. If you live on campus and your campus offers this service, it's worthwhile to purchase any equipment you need to connect directly—the connection will be much faster and more reliable than any other means of Internet connection. Usually all you'll need is an Ethernet card and a login name and password.

Dial-up Access. If you don't live on campus, or if your dorm isn't wired for direct access, then you must connect via dial-up access. You'll need a modem for your computer and access to a phone line. Contact your computer services department to learn the dial-in phone number and to obtain a login name and password. If your school doesn't have a dial-in number, you can still get Internet access by subscribing to an **Internet service provider**. These services will often offer a flat monthly rate for unlimited Internet access, usually around twenty dollars per month. Some of the most popular Internet service providers are AT&T, Earthlink, Mindspring, and America Online.

URLs: Addresses on the Internet

The Internet has no center. There is no single computer or group of computers in the "middle" of the Internet. There isn't even a "map" or physical representation of how all the computers on the Internet are connected. The only thing everyone on the Internet has agreed upon is how resources are named. Every resource on the Internet has a unique name, different from every other resource on the Internet. Once you know a resource's name, you don't need to know where it is, what kind of computer it's on, or how to get there. All the information you need to find every resource on the Internet is included in the name itself.

Names on the Internet are called **URLs** (Uniform Resource Locators). A URL has several parts:

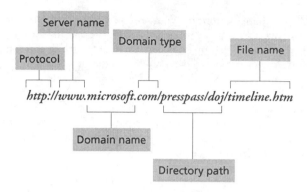

The **protocol** indicates the type of link to be made with the server. In this case, it's *http:*, which stands for hypertext transfer protocol—the protocol used for all resources on the World Wide Web. The **domain** name is registered by the Web site owner, in this case the Microsoft Corporation. The **server name** (usually *www* for Web sites) refers to the server the site owner uses to host the Web site. The **domain type** indicates what type of organization the owner is, here a commercial organization. The **directory path** reflects the overall organization of the Web site. This resource is located in the *doj* subdirectory of the *corpinfo* **directory**. The **file name** is the name the site owner has given to the particular resource you're looking at, here a timeline of the Department of Justice's investigation of Microsoft for possible antitrust violations. Note that slashes (not backslashes, as in DOS directories) are used to separate directory names from each other and from the domain name and file name. Two slashes are used to separate the protocol from the domain name.

When you pronounce a URL, you can save time by using a few common conventions. If the person you're speaking to knows you're referring to a Web address, you can leave out the *http://.* Then say, "www dot microsoft dot com slash corpinfo slash doj slash timeline dot htm." Make sure you spell out any words with unconventional spellings. However, when you refer to URLs in formal research, always give the complete URL.

NETIQUETTE TIP

Netiquette: Netiquette is a system of online manners based on common sense and the limitations of the Internet. Throughout this book, look for these tips to help you present a polished image on the Net.

Chapter 2

E-Mail

Using e-mail in your research

You can use e-mail in any of the following ways:

- To connect with members of the class on an individual basis and with the instructor outside of class and office hours. E-mail can be especially useful when an unexpected problem or question arises, or when other settings are inappropriate or uncomfortable for asking the question.
- To send inquiries to the instructor, for example if you have missed class or have a question about an assignment.
- To turn in papers or other homework, to which instructors can respond by e-mailing comments back to you.
- To obtain resources for a research a project, from **listservs** (see page 18), the **World Wide Web** (see Chapter 3), other students, or your instructor.
- To conduct online "interviews" or surveys to gather data for your research.

E-mail is also an invaluable tool for collaborating with others:

- You can e-mail peer review partners drafts and comments with the advantage of being able to ask questions and carry on a dialogue.
- When working on collective projects with a small group, you can use e-mail to brainstorm about ideas, share work you have completed individually, or coordinate times to meet as a group.

- You can e-mail resources and materials that you have found to students who have similar research topics.

How e-mail works

Electronic mail (e-mail) is the basic technology that allows you to communicate with other people on the Internet. E-mail uses the power of computers to bring humans closer together. You can send e-mail messages to a single instructor or student, a group of students, the class as a whole, a campus e-mail **discussion list**, or a worldwide audience made up of personal contacts or subscribers to a **listserv**. By subscribing to a listserv, you can observe and even participate in international discussions among experts in nearly any field you can imagine. You can use e-mail to coordinate group work for your class, or exchange messages with your instructor and your friends.

The basic tool for sending and receiving e-mail is called a **mailreader** (also known as a "mail client"). While it may be possible to exchange e-mail without a mailreader, these programs provide an easy interface for reading, composing, posting, and **downloading** e-mail messages. Common mailreaders include Eudora (for Macintosh systems) and Weudora (for Windows and DOS systems). The major World Wide Web **browsers**, Netscape Navigator and Microsoft Internet Explorer, also include mailreaders. It is also easy to find many other mailreaders with different features and characteristics. Many mailreader programs can be downloaded from the Internet as **freeware** (software programs distributed free of charge).

Mailreaders send and receive messages through **mail servers**, programs on computers connected to the Internet which organize, store, and distribute e-mail messages to various users. Servers exchange with each other (often through a chain of several servers in different locations across the country or worldwide) using two-part e-mail **addresses**.

Addresses and their elements

A typical e-mail address contains two elements. The **mailbox name** or **user's name** appears before the **@** sign (pronounced "at"), and the **domain** information, representing the server that provides e-mail to the user, follows the @ sign. A sample message might use these addresses:

```
From: dmunger-dtc@mindspring.com
To: president@whitehouse.gov
```

The mailbox name of the sender is *dmunger-dtc*. The recipient's mailbox name is *president*.

The domain generally contains information about the organization and organization type. Elements of the domain are separated by a period (.) generally called a dot. Here, the sender's domain includes the name of the organization, *mindspring*, and an abbreviation describing the type of organization, *com* (commercial). The mailbox of the recipient, president, is registered with the organization *whitehouse*, classified as *gov* (government).

In the United States, the standard domain types are:

```
.edu = educational institution
.com = commercial organization
.gov = government organization
.mil = military institution
.org = non-profit organization
.net = (often) Internet service provider
```

Outside the United States, domain names usually end in a two-letter element indicating the country of origin: for example, *.jp* (Japan), *.nl* (the Netherlands), and *.eg* (Egypt).

Many mailreaders allow you to save addresses in a file called an address book, which makes it unnecessary to retype an address. You can even assign more than one address to each entry (often called a **nickname**) in your address book, so you can send e-mail to many people simply by typing one entry in your e-mail message. For example, if you are working on a group project in English 101, you could create an address book entry called "Eng_101_group" to instantly send a message to everyone in your group.

Getting connected

We recommend that all students set up an e-mail account. Most colleges and universities have already incorporated computer and Internet fees into tuition costs, so they generally offer "free" or very inexpensive e-mail accounts to students and faculty. Although some students will inevitably have problems along the way, setting up an account is usually a fairly simple process. For more information on Internet connection, see pages 8–9.

Setting up an e-mail account may take a little time, so request your account very early in the term. Learn about your systems by reading any handouts with detailed step-by-step instructions. Since schools frequently change e-mail procedures from term to term as they expand their computer services, bear in mind that some of the instructions may be incorrect. To verify that your account is working, send yourself a test message.

Using your e-mail program

Most people send and receive e-mail messages using an e-mail program on a personal computer. The e-mail program can talk to mail servers, which are programs on Internet-connected machines that store and distribute electronic messages.

E-mail programs (Eudora is probably the most popular and is available as freeware) allow you to both compose messages to send to others and retrieve mail from the mail server and bring it to your machine. You can even send and receive files you created using another program such as Microsoft Word or Adobe Photoshop.

In Eudora (Figure 2.1), by clicking on items across the top bar, you can automatically save a copy of the message in your "out" mailbox and control whether or not to use your **signature file** (which Eudora saves for you in another window—see page 22). The Queue button prepares this message for mailing, but the outgoing message will not be sent until the user selects a menu command to send all his

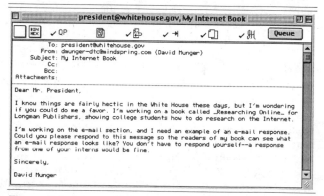

Figure 2.1: An e-mail message composed on Eudora

or her queued messages. This feature is useful if you want to minimize the time you are actually connected to the Internet (if a modem and a phone share the same line, for example, or your Internet access is billed by the minute). You can easily change your mail setting to deliver the message immediately if you prefer.

Before you can use it to send and receive messages, you need to tell your e-mail program how to access your account. In Eudora, your account information is kept in the Settings panel. Other programs may keep this information in the Preferences panel. Your campus computer services department or Internet service provider should give you the correct information to input when you register your account. Here is an example of a Settings panel that has been configured to send and receive mail.

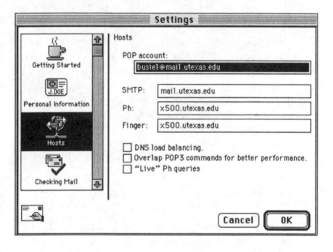

Once you set up the information you will never have to retype your e-mail address, your signature file, or other information. Of course, you will always have access to the configurations, so you can modify the program's settings to your liking.

E-mail conventions

By its nature, e-mail tends to be less formal than regular mail ("snail mail"). Some have suggested that e-mail compares more closely with spoken conversation than formal letter writing. That's probably a good thing, because it allows people to concentrate on getting their message across quickly instead of focusing on decorum. However, you should still take care when composing a message, because unlike spoken conversation, an e-mail message cannot convey the subtle nuances of speech such as intonation and facial expression.

A debate is currently raging about whether messages should contain unedited typographical errors and abbreviations like *BTW* ("by the way"), *FWIW* ("for what it's worth") or *IMHO* ("in my humble opinion"), *msg* ("message"), *mtg* ("meeting"), or *shd* ("should"). One side of the argument suggests that the immediacy of e-mail is diminished when writers must take time to follow all the rigors of academic writing. Others argue that the development of an Internet "code" of communication unnecessarily excludes people who aren't "in the know" while offering a convenient excuse for those who haven't made the effort to learn to communicate properly.

NETIQUETTE TIP

E-mail language: When in doubt, use conservative language in your e-mail messages. Don't use short-cuts like *BTW* or *IMHO* unless you're sure your recipients understand what the abbreviations mean and you know them well enough to address them by their first names.

Another e-mail convention arose because of the ease with which computer technology reproduces text. When you **reply** to an e-mail message, you can usually include the original message in the response (see Figure 2.2 for an example). The text that is quoted from the original message is denoted with an **angle bracket** (>) before each line of text. Most e-mail programs automatically quote the whole text of the preceding message into their reply, so reply quotations can get quite long with little or no effort of your own. Some e-mail programs such as Microsoft Outlook and Netscape Communicator format quotes differently. Be sure to learn how your e-mail program formats quotes so you understand where the information in an e-mail message is coming from.

In most e-mail programs, each time you quote a message an additional angle bracket will appear before each line. This

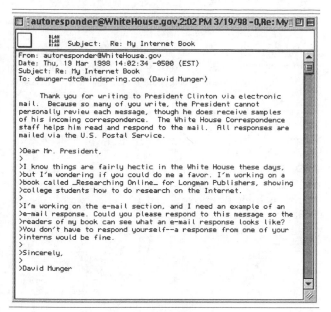

Figure 2.2: An example of an e-mail with a reply quotation

nesting of quotations continues until one reader decides that there is no need to include the older text, and deletes it. Because e-mail messages are read with varying frequency by different users, you may want to include the original question or issue for clarity. It can be useful to "overhear" part of the original conversation or to analyze the original message a second time. Make sure you contextualize the material you quote in your response.

Netiquette Tip

E-mail reply quotations: An unnecessarily long reply quotation can be an annoyance to your recipient. To save space and time, delete the portions of a reply quotation that are no longer relevant.

Remember to protect the privacy of your correspondents. Don't send someone else's e-mail message to another person without the author's permission. When working in a group, it's a good idea to agree in advance that everyone in the group can freely forward work to the others.

What is a listserv?

A **listserv**, also known as a "mailing list" or "list," is a program which allows e-mail to be sent to a group of addresses simultaneously. (Throughout this text we will use the term *listserv* generically to denote a range of mailing list programs including Listserv, Majordomo, and Listproc.) Though listservs vary according to function, type, and administration, each listserv defines a narrow subject area which all posts are expected to fall within. For example, the discussion list *MODBRITS* carefully defines its scope as "Modern British and Irish Literature: 1895–1955," and participants are expected to abide by the list's geographic and chronological limits or provide a good rationale for ranging outside them.

NETIQUETTE TIP

Listserv messages: Don't send a message to a list just to pass the time or to try to sell a car (unless the list is for the purpose of selling used cars). For most lists, posts like this would be frowned upon and might result in a number of angry messages (or **flames**) from list members. Some lists have moderators who screen messages before sending them to the full list in order to ensure their relevance. Repeated inflammatory or "off-topic" messages from a user can result in removal from the list. Remember that your message is going to a large audience. Ask yourself if your message is likely to be useful to all the members of the list. Also remember that your issue may have been discussed before you became a member of the list.

Make sure you follow a listserv discussion for a period of time to clarify the nature of the listserv's audience and learn what constitutes an interesting or convincing message on that list. Sometimes, the boundaries of allowable topics on a list are very narrowly defined. For example, the *h-latam* list (a discussion of Latin American history) specifically defines its subject to exclude current events in Latin America. Because the list sees its function as providing a level-headed discussion of "historical" events, especially as these relate to teaching history, potentially heated political discussions of more recent events in Latin America are discouraged. A post discussing causes and effects of the Zapatista uprising in Chiapas, Mexico, for instance, would not be allowed on the list unless it was directed solely to bibliographic source material or pedagogical concerns.

For gathering substantive research material, the most useful lists are those posting items like news stories, articles, documents, and expert commentary. However, you should not give up on a list simply because it focuses on discussion, for you can learn a lot by keeping track of and participating in active listserv debates. You will see how opinions are formed, revised, and complicated, and how multiple perspectives can inform a topic.

Along with the research possibilities provided by listservs, e-mail can be an effective tool for transferring and gathering other types of information. For instance, many online library catalogs and databases allow users to mail information to their accounts. When you find a useful online article, for instance, you can easily e-mail yourself the material. Once you receive the article in electronic form, you can refer back to the piece at a later date or cut and paste quotations into your paper (with proper acknowledgment, of course).

Use listservs to initiate research conversations

Your instructor may create class listservs or **nicknames** to make announcements, revise reading or meeting schedules, forward supplementary material, start discussion, or ask for feedback on a particular topic. Lists and nicknames also give you the opportunity to contribute material for course reading and to share relevant resources with the entire class.

Joining conversations outside of the classroom will illustrate your commitment to discussing issues and ideas, and will demonstrate the importance of your writing in a larger context/forum. Using listservs can give you access to the opinions of experts. This access to information is a useful stimulus for creating a topic and finding a way to enter a conversation. For example, depending on the listserv, you might come across an index of sources about a research topic or gather current information on a contemporary debate or event.

Besides drawing on the conversations of subscribers to a list, you can ask questions, post your own opinions, and receive reactions to the arguments you are developing for class. Don't expect the list to write your paper for you or answer obvious questions. If you post a message like "Can anyone out there help me with my *Hamlet* paper?" or "What was the name of the guy who wrote *Catcher in the Rye*?" you will likely receive some hostile responses and few, if any, useful replies. But if you are able to engage the audience with either an interesting argument or an important category of research or analysis, you will likely receive many useful citations and suggestions for further thought. Of course, you can easily save all of these messages on a diskette and retrieve them when you need them. You can also forward messages to an instructor, other students, or people outside the classroom.

How to subscribe to a listserv

Finding listservs on your research topic

The easiest way to find a listserv is to do a search on the **World Wide Web** (see Chapter 3 for more information on browsing the Web). Point your browser to a mailing list **search engine** like *http://www.liszt.com/* or *http://tile.net /lists/*. There, you can search using **keywords** appropriate to your topic or browse through directories of mailing lists that may be of interest to you.

If you're not sure about a listserv, just subscribe to it for a few days to see if it's useful. If it's not useful to you, you can easily unsubscribe.

Subscribing to a listserv

Subscribing to a listserv is complicated by the fact that there are three major types of listservs: **Listserv**, **Listproc**, and **Majordomo**. Fortunately, it's easy to distinguish between the three types, because the address you e-mail to subscribe always begins with either *listserv, listproc,* or *majordomo*. Never type anything in the subject line, regardless of the type of list you're subscribing to.

Listserv. To subscribe to this type of list, send e-mail to the administrative address for the list you want to subscribe to. For example, if you want to subscribe to the African American Women's Literature list, you send the following e-mail message:

```
To: listserv@cmuvm.csv.cmich.edu
subscribe AAWOMLIT your name
```

Don't literally type "your name," unless that's what it says on your birth certificate. If your name is Fred Jones, type that in place of *your name*. The convention in this book is to indicate where you need to fill in your own information by using *italic* type. By the way, one of the most common mistakes beginning computer users make is to literally type in everything they see in the documentation. Whenever you're learning a new program, take a moment to see if the documentation has a special way of indicating information you need to provide yourself—usually, you'll find the going much easier.

Listproc. Subscribing to a listproc works the same way as a listserv. For example, to subscribe to the listproc American Literature, send the following e-mail:

```
To: listproc@lists.missouri.edu
subscribe AMLIT-L your name
```

Majordomo. Since Majordomo servers aren't as sophisticated as Listserv or Listproc, you usually need to include your e-mail address in the subscribe message. For example, to subscribe to the Postcolonial list, send the following e-mail:

```
To: majordomo@jefferson.village.virginia.edu
subscribe postcolonial your e-mail address
```

Unsubscribing to a listserv

To unsubscribe from the lists above, send the following messages:

Listserv

```
To: listserv@cmuvm.csv.cmich.edu
signoff AAWOMLIT
```

Listproc

```
To: listproc@lists.missouri.edu
signoff AMLIT-L
```

Majordomo

```
To: majordomo@jefferson.village.virginia.edu
unsubscribe postcolonial your e-mail address
```

Emoticons and other e-mail miscellany

Many Internet users attempt to express sarcasm and light-hearted emotion by using **emoticons** (usually called **smileys**). Smileys are roughly the Internet equivalent of a wink, and about as sophisticated. Though they often denote a lack of careful writing, smileys sometimes help clarify the author's intention. The basic smiley is a sideways happy face :-) (tilt your head to the left to read it), although a host of others can be used to express a broad range of emotions (see Table 2.1). Though a writer might incorporate a smiley in informal prose, it would be preferable in a formal composition to use words to convey irony effectively. Remember, if you say something truly offensive, adding a smiley after it isn't going to do a lot to cool down the offended party.

Another way of personalizing e-mail communication is by adding a **signature** or **sig file** to a message. A signature is a section of text automatically appended to the bottom of e-mail messages. Signatures serve as a way to identify the author and place him/her socially, professionally, and personally. Besides supplying the writer's e-mail address to facilitate replies, a signature will often carry a writer's professional or academic affil-

:-)	basic smiley
;-)	winking happy smiley
;-(	crying smiley
:-{	mustache
:-}X	bow-tie-wearing smiley
@:-}	smiley just back from the hairdresser
C=:-)	chef smiley
8(:-)	Mickey Mouse
:——}	you lie like pinnochio
[:-)	smiley wearing a walkman
X:-)	little kid with a propeller beanie

Table 2.1: **A small sampling of smileys**
Taken from *ftp://ftp.wwa.com/pub/Scarecrow/Misc/Smilies*

iations, an indication of whether the current message is personal or professional, or a favorite quotation. To lighten this rather dry information, many authors have developed elaborate arrangements of text and symbols in their signatures.

Although widespread, signature files have not been entirely accepted by all Internet users. As a result, plays upon the signature file abound. One of the most succinct signature files, dutifully attached at the end of many messages, is "This is not a signature."

Chapter 3

The World Wide Web

Using the World Wide Web in your research

You can begin to answer countless questions simply by doing a search of the millions of resources available over the **World Wide Web**. The Web has become the single most significant Internet resource because of its tremendous flexibility and its incredible ease of use. How flexible is it? *All* of the other Internet resources described in the rest of this book can be duplicated using the Web's protocol and interface. How easy is it? If you can point a mouse and click a button, you can use the Web.

When you begin a research project, start by thinking about the ways in which the Web might be able to help. For example, if you are writing a paper on the importance of gender in Shakespeare's *Hamlet,* you can search the Web for online commentary on this issue. You can locate experts who may be able to help you find other resources on the subject. You can even use the Web to locate printed resources in your school library, as well as other resources that may be available via interlibrary loan.

If you are creating a Web page on pollution in the Ganges River in India, you can look for updates on the problem from global environmental agencies. You can find reports on the issue from online news services. You can locate other Web sites devoted to the same issue or related issues. You can request copies of journal articles on the subject to be faxed directly to you.

Even though the Internet is vastly different from traditional research sources, you can still follow the same steps when using the Internet as a research tool as when you use a traditional library. You still need to narrow your topic, refine searches, and evaluate source materials. Here's a summary of how the Internet can be used with the steps in a traditional research project.

- **Finding a topic.** Surf the Web or perform keyword searches (see below) as you brainstorm on possible topics.
- **Narrowing and refining the topic.** Once you settle on a broad topic, you can run a more extensive set of keyword searches can help narrow and refine your topic.
- **Finding and evaluating sources.** When you have chosen a topic, review the Web sites you visited while refining the topic. Determine whether they now offer new information, and investigate any promising new links. Perform additional keyword searches relating to all aspects of your project. Look for sites that refer to your sources (both online and other) to see what others have said about them.

What is the World Wide Web?

Now you know what the Web can *do;* here's what the Web *is.* Most simply, the World Wide Web is a communication system that delivers **hypermedia** built on the Internet's global network of computers. Hypermedia is an extension of **hypertext**. A hypertext document is text designed to be easily and richly linked to itself and to other hypertext documents. Hypermedia expands on that concept by including other media, such as audio, video, pictures, databases, and animation. Both hypertext and hypermedia can be incredibly powerful in the way they multiply the possible associations to a given piece of information. By connecting hypermedia documents to the amazing computing resources of the Internet, the World Wide Web magnifies that power exponentially.

World Wide Web documents are designed to be viewed using computer programs called **browsers**. The two most popular browsers are Microsoft Internet Explorer and Netscape Navigator (most people just say "Netscape" to refer to both Navigator and its newer cousin, Communicator). Each file on the World Wide Web is assigned an address called a **Uniform Resource Locator**

(**URL**—see page 9), which tells the browser the exact location of the file. Files are stored on Web servers which are equipped with software that enables documents to be linked and shared.

The World Wide Web is revolutionary because it allows connections between documents regardless of their location. A single Web page might link to a sound file at an **FTP** site in Australia, a text file at a Gopher site in Europe, and a graphic file at a Web server in Idaho. In addition, most Web browsers now incorporate Internet technologies, like **Gopher** (see page 65) and **newsgroups** (see Chapter 5), which once required specialized software to access.

Browsing on the Web

So how do you visit a **Web site**? All you need to do is connect to the Internet (see Chapter 1), run your browser program, and type the site's URL into the "location" box of your browser. The site will appear on your monitor.

You can visit the many sites listed in this book in this way. You can also visit any site you may have learned about from another resource—your instructor, a book, an advertisement, or a friend. You can use these same techniques to view information from around the world. If you're doing a report on pollution in the Ganges River in India, you might visit the site shown in Figure 3.1. You can visit related Web pages by clicking on **links** (usually underlined text) on each page you visit. In the example, you can visit a site with information about Varanasi, India by moving your mouse to point the cursor arrow at the text "VARANASI, India." The cursor arrow then turns into a pointing finger, as shown. This indicates that the text "VARANASI, India" is **hot**, meaning that something will happen if you click on it. Just click, and you will be transported to a different site. This sample Web site also includes many other types of hot spots. Clicking the banner advertisement at the top of the page will take you to a site promoting CNN's new Portuguese Web site. On the left side of the page is an **imagemap**, which can take you to many different places, depending on where you click on the image. To find out if a given area of a page is hot, just move the arrow over that space. If the arrow turns into a pointing hand, then clicking will transport you to another Web page.

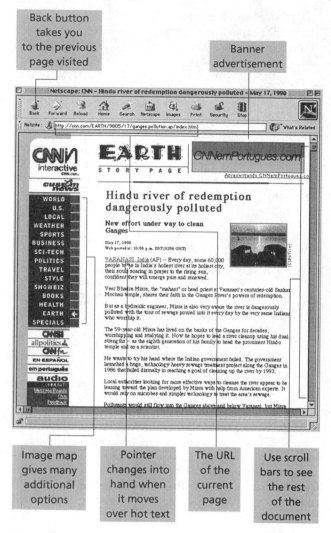

Back button takes you to the previous page visited

Banner advertisement

Image map gives many additional options

Pointer changes into hand when it moves over hot text

The URL of the current page

Use scroll bars to see the rest of the document

Figure 3.1: A sample page on the World Wide Web

Links are what give the Web its tremendous power. By connecting different media such as sound, text, and images, as well entirely different Web sites from around the world, they give you the power to create a media-rich environment that can't be duplicated in any other way. You can travel around the world and back simply by clicking on the links of the Web pages you visit. That brings up a potential problem. You could be reading a very interesting Web page about pollution in the Ganges, and then click on a link that discusses the Hindu religion. Click on a link on that page, and you're at a site discussing the influence of Mahatma Gandhi. Interesting stuff, but weren't you writing a report on pollution in the Ganges? Fortunately, all Web browsers have a Back button, which simply takes you to the previous page you visited. Click again, and it takes you to the page before that. Decide you really do want to know about Gandhi? No problem, just click on Forward until you return to that site.

One warning: the Back button has limited powers. If you visit a site you think will be useful in your research, make a note of its URL. You can do this automatically by using a powerful feature offered by browsers like Navigator: the **Bookmark** command (Note: This book gives only Navigator commands; see Table 3.1 for the Explorer equivalent). Bookmarks allow you to save the URLs of sites you've found to be particularly useful so you can easily find them later. You can even organize your bookmarks into folders according to different research topics.

NETIQUETTE TIP

Using bookmarks on public computers: When you're using a public computer, save your bookmarks to a diskette so the computer's bookmarks menu doesn't get cluttered by dozens of users' personal bookmarks, and so you can use them on a different computer. In Navigator, you save bookmarks by first choosing Bookmarks from the Windows menu, then choosing Save as from the File menu.

Searching the Web

When you use a browser for the first time, you almost invariably will be pointed to a **search engine** or **subject directory**. These are simply Web sites which allow you to search for the particular resources you're looking for on the World Wide Web. With a search engine, you can type a word or set of words, and it will present you with a list of sites where that word appears. With subject directory, you search for sites by selecting from lists of subjects. Gradually, you narrow the subject lists to the topic that interests you.

Netscape term	Explorer equivalent
Location	Address
Bookmarks	Favorites
Save As	Export
Open Bookmark File	Import
Reload	Refresh
Back	Back
Forward	Forward
Stop	Stop
Monopoly	Innovation

Table 3.1: Netscape Navigator terms and their Microsoft Internet Explorer equivalents

While it may be easiest to simply perform your search with the search tool that comes up when you load your browser, you should realize that you have many more resources available. The only reason you see the search tool you do is because the search tool company has paid the company that makes your browser a lot of money. It's important to identify the search tool that works best for the type of resources you need. To learn more about subject directories, see below. For more on search engines, see page 32.

Searching with Web subject directories

Web subject directories are good places to begin a research project. People, often experts in a field, create subject directories by visiting a huge number of sites, then grouping together relevant sites with similar topics.

You can use a subject directory to help decide on a research project through a process called **tunneling**. When you visit a subject directory, you are presented with a list of general topics. You click on the topic that interests you, and a list of subtopics appears. You can continue selecting subtopics until you arrive at a list of Web sites on your specific topic. Then you can read the site's description and decide if it's relevant to your project.

When you've decided on a topic and are conducting indepth research, subject directories can still be useful. You can type in a keyword and search through the subject headings to locate sites indexed by your subject directory, or use tunnelling to locate additional sources.

Searching with Yahoo!

Yahoo! (*http://www.yahoo.com/*) is one of the oldest and most valuable Web searching tools. For more subject directories, see pages 37–38. Dozens of workers at Yahoo! visit thousands of Web sites every day and place them in a hierarchical index, providing descriptions and even reviews of the sites they list (see Figure 3.2). Yahoo! can and does often reject a site from its index if it doesn't believe the site to be a valuable or unique resource. (This doesn't necessarily mean *useful:* Yahoo! lists close to a hundred "cam" sites that simply show live pictures of some relatively benign room or object deemed worthy of attention by bored computer hackers, such as the coffee pot in a research lab or the infamous Netscape Fish-Cam.)

You can use both tunneling and searching to find Web sites on Yahoo! For example, if you were doing a project on

Figure 3.2: A subject directory in Yahoo!

coral reefs, you could either follow the menus supplied by Yahoo! to locate sites, or your could simply type `coral reefs` in the `Search` box on the Yahoo! home page. Figure 3.2 shows the results of clicking in the "coral reefs" subdirectory in Yahoo!

Yahoo!'s biggest strength—human indexers—is also its biggest weakness. What a Yahoo! employee deems irrelevant may be completely relevant to you. You have no way of knowing what's been left out by the human indexer. Yahoo! has also become more commercialized over the years, and occasionally it may point you in the direction of a paid sponsor rather than toward legitimate academic resources.

Searching with Web search engines

Instead of relying on humans to catalog a select (if still very large) list of sites, search engines (often called **robots**) try to automate the process and provide a way of searching the entire Web.

Use search engines when you need to perform a thorough search of the Web's resources. Search engines use computers to index the Web, so they are not limited to the sites human indexers locate. The AltaVista search engine indexes over 900 million Web sites. By typing `Shakespeare`, for example, you can find every site in the index which includes that word anywhere in its text. Of course using "Shakespeare" as a keyword will generate several million hits, from bookstores to academic sites to car dealers. You'll need to select a few more keywords to narrow your search.

Searching with AltaVista

Perhaps the most ambitious robot search engine, AltaVista (*http://www.altavista.com/*) attempts to catalog the entire Web by periodically visiting every known site and adding key elements of the site's text to its database. When you type in a keyword, it scans its database according to a predetermined set of rules and gives you a list of the results.

Figure 3.3 shows the results of a student's search for sites with the keywords "gender," "Shakespeare," and "Hamlet." This search returned over 800,000 Web pages! Unfortunately, because the search was performed by a "dumb" robot, many of the sites listed are not relevant to the student's research project.

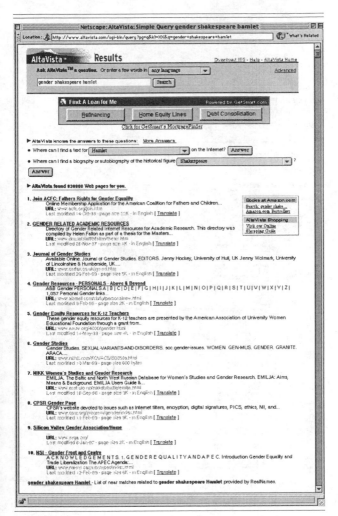

Figure 3.3: A basic keyword search using AltaVista

AltaVista offers a solution: the "domain" feature. Figure 3.4 shows the results of refining this search to include only sites with the "edu" domain type—only sites hosted by educational institutions. Though this search returned "only" 173,000 documents, many more of them were relevant to this student's research question.

AltaVista offers many other features to help you find exactly what you're looking for. The best way to learn about

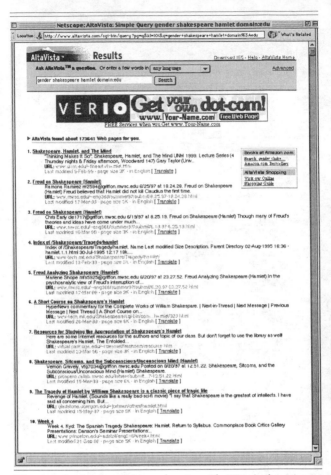

Figure 3.4: A keyword search using AltaVista's domain feature

them is probably just to try them out for yourself. Visit the AltaVista help page at ***http://www.altavista.com/av/content/help.htm*** for more features to help refine your search.

One word of caution regarding searching with AltaVista and a growing number of commercial Internet search engines. Because AltaVista is a for-profit enterprise, it is constantly changing as it seeks new ways to profit from its position on the Web. One obvious way it does this is through advertising. It's easy to avoid banner ads if you're not interested, but other ads may not be as obvious. At this writing, for example, AltaVista was testing a program where advertising clients pay to have their listing appear first when you search using a term they specify. Be aware of these and other sorts of commercial messages as you work—remember, your job is to find the best sources for your project, not those that have paid the most to get noticed.

Searching with Lycos

Lycos (*http://www.lycos.com/*) is David's new favorite search robot because of its uncluttered interface and (usually) quick downloads. It works in much the same way as AltaVista, but offers a few additional options.

The most useful feature of Lycos is its advanced search function at *http://lycospro.lycos.com*. For the Ganges River project, just typing "Ganges River pollution" in the search engine window leads to a variety of Web pages, some more useful than others. Using the advanced search feature as shown in Figure 3.5, this student was able to specify the order in which Lycos sorted the results, by placing a "high" priority on matching all the words, how frequently the words appeared, and how early in the document they appeared. You can see the result of this search in Figure 3.6.

Figure 3.5: The advanced search screen of Lycos

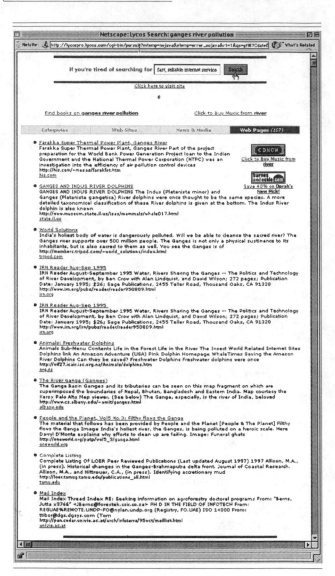

Figure 3.6: Advanced search results in Lycos

Another useful feature of the Lycos advanced search is the ability to search within specified sites. For example, if you noticed that the University of Pennsylvania's site had a particularly valuable collection of Asian art, you could specify to search only within the domain *upenn.edu*. You can also specify to search only within Lycos's "Top 5%," a list of sites reviewed by Lycos editors.

Searching with other services

There are literally hundreds of other search services out there. Rather than give a lengthy description of each one, we simply provide a selection of their URLs with a brief note or two on the most popular.

Search engines (robots)
Excite
http://excite.com/
Attempts to avoid "**spam**" by ignoring keywords specified by Web site designers—success of this approach is debatable.

WebCrawler
http://webcrawler.com/
Easy to use, comprehensive. Gives just the Web page title—no descriptions.

Infoseek
http://infoseek.go.com/
Relatively fast. Allows you to easily search the results of a preceding search.

Savvy Search
http://savvysearch.com/
Allows you to search over one hundred engines simultaneously. A bit slow, but useful if you're having difficulty finding anything at all on your topic.

Ask Jeeves
http://www.askjeeves.com/
Surprisingly useful. Designed for beginners, it offers quick answers to many common questions, such as "How do I apply for a passport?"

Mamma
http://www.mamma.com/

HotBot
http://www.hotbot.com/

Subject directory indexes
Many of the search engines listed above, including AltaVista and Infoseek, now include subject directory options as well. Here are some additional, more academically oriented subject directories.

The Internet Public Library
http://www.ipl.org/
A subject directory created by librarians to mimick the organization of a library; very rationally and intuitively structured.

Library of Congress World Wide Web Home Page
http://lcWeb.loc.gov/
Search the entire Library of Congress catalog, an extensive online photo database, and more.

WWW Virtual Library
http://www.vlib.org
An index divided into hundreds of categories. Each category is managed by a specialist, so categories are variable in quality, depending on the particular specialist.

The Argus Clearinghouse
http://www.clearinghouse.net/

Advanced Web searches

Boolean searches

Most of the engines for keyword searches allow you to use some form of **Boolean** (logical) operators to modify search strings. Employing these commands allows you to narrow a search and to bring back a smaller number of **hits**. Hits are simply listings of Web pages containing the search terms you specify. Here are some of the basic commands—as it turns out, the same commands you use for the various library databases (such as the MLA online index).

Entering	Searches for
`pizza soda chips`	all sites containing the terms *pizza, soda,* or *chips*
`pizza AND soda`	only sites containing both the terms *pizza* and *soda*
`pizza OR chips`	either *pizza* or *chips* (note that *OR* is usually necessary only when combining Boolean operators)
`pizza NOT anchovies`	only sites containing the term *pizza* but not the term *anchovies*

`pizza*`	occurrences of the root within other words: pizzas, pizzacatto, etc. (a **fuzzy search** of *pizza*)
`"Chicago style pizza"`	only occurrences of all three terms together (a **literal search**)
`Mario Andretti`	Many search engines will consider any two capitalized words a **name search** and return only occurrences of the two terms together.

Boolean operators can also be used together. Used in combination, they offer tremendous power. For the most predictable results, use parentheses to enclose the Boolean operation you want the search engine to execute first. For example, the search pattern

```
(racial OR sexual) AND (discrimination OR bias)
```

would produce a list of Web pages containing any combination the following terms, in any order: *racial* and *discrimination, sexual* and *discrimination, racial* and *bias, sexual* and *bias* (but not any other pages containing only one of the terms, or combinations like *racial* and *sexual*).

Not every search engine uses Boolean operators in exactly the same way. For more on Boolean searching, check out Advanced Searching Techniques at ***http://www.learnthenet.com/english/html/77advanc.htm***

Using the Link command

Another useful command available on some search engines is the Link command. Suppose you want to know every Web site that links to the Microsoft Department of Justice Timeline. Simply type the following in the AltaVista search engine, then press the `search` button.

```
link:http://www.microsoft.com/presspass/doj
/timeline.htm
```

AltaVista will list all the Web pages in its database that contain a link back to the Microsoft Timeline page. You can also use the Link command on Infoseek.

The Link command is a good way to find additional sources relevant to your topic, as well as sites that critique, analyze, or respond to a page you're interested in.

Searching for individuals

Many search engines and indexes, including Yahoo! and Excite, have "yellow pages" options that allow you to search for an individual's e-mail or physical address. The only problem with this function is that you usually need to know more than an individual's name in order to be sure you've got the right person. Suppose you type `John Smith` into Yahoo!'s yellow pages—you could end up with hundreds of listings.

In academic research, you may be interested in finding a faculty member at a college or university. In this case, it may be easier to go directly to that institution's home page and look for a "search" function. How do you find the institution's URL? Do a Yahoo! search.

Advanced browsing techniques

Search engines aren't the only way to locate information on the Web. Many times, you can get better results by exploiting the structure of a URL. URLs have several different components, and each component can lead you to a different place. Consider the URL for Microsoft's Department of Justice Timeline:

http://www.microsoft.com/presspass/doj/timeline.htm

The directory path consists of narrower and narrower subject divisions within the domain *microsoft.com*. If you want to find out additional press information about Microsoft, you could go to a search engine like Lycos and run an additional search, or you could simply delete the text *doj/timeline.htm* from the location box in your browser, and press `Enter`. That would take you to an index of the presspass directory, which contains many more links to Microsoft corporate information intended for the press.

You can often speed up your browsing by taking advantage of the fact that large institutions usually have easily remembered domain names. For example, you could perform a Yahoo! search to look for Harvard University's Web site, or you could make an educated guess: just type `http://www.harvard.edu` in your browser's location box. In fact, both Navigator and Explorer will accept partial URLs—just `www.harvard.edu` works fine. If you're looking for a corporate site, these browsers will even guess the server name and domain type correctly. Typing just `microsoft` will bring up *http://www.microsoft.com/*.

Other research sites

News sites

Using search engines alone won't direct you to some of the most valuable sites on the Web. Internet search engines generally only index Web sites—not the information contained in databases located on the Web. Most major newspapers, news magazines, and television news networks have huge, searchable Web sites that allow you to find an immense array of documents on news events. Articles, photos, and other documents from these sites may not be indexed by the major search engines, so the only way to locate these documents is to go directly to the source. Many newspapers charge a fee for searching past issues, but one that doesn't as of press time for this volume is the *Seattle Times*.

Some newspaper and magazine sites

New York Times
http://www.nytimes.com/

Washington Post
http://www.washingtonpost.com/

Seattle Times
http://www.seattletimes.com/

Time Magazine
http://pathfinder.com/time/

Some television news sites

MSNBC
http://msnbc.com/

CNN
http://cnn.com/

ABC
http://www.abcnews.com/

Encyclopedia sites

Most encyclopedias on the Web charge a subscription fee of from five to ten dollars a month (for individuals). However, your institution may have a subscription already. If it does, you may be able to access the following Web encyclopedias for free. Encarta offers a free abridged version that gives you a paragraph or two of text instead of the full article for each listing.

Encarta
http://encarta.msn.com/

Encyclopedia Britannica
http://www.eb.com/

Grolier
http://www.grolier.com/

Library sites

Most major learning institutions now have searchable indexes of their holdings on the World Wide Web. If your own institution has such a site, it may also give you access to additional resources available only to students and faculty at your institution, such as searchable indexes like *The Readers Guide to Periodical Literature*, *The MLA Index*, and others. If you don't find what you need on your own institution's site, try searching the catalogs from other institutions. You can often request holdings from other schools via your own library's interlibrary loan department.

Chapter 4

Managing Web Site Information

As your research progresses, you'll begin to access a tremendous amount of material. It's temptingly easy to download everything about a particular topic. Before long, you'll end up with collection of printouts and files that makes no more sense than the vague ideas you had when you began your project. In order for your research to be effective, you need a plan for managing the information you find.

When you start a project, you'll want to skim a few online sources to get a sense of the broad context of your chosen research topic. As you work, make a note of the sources that you think will be useful later on when you begin to learn more about your topic. You can quickly evaluate a source's usefulness by using your browser's Find command to look for a few key terms that you know are important.

Later, as you focus and narrow your topic, you will want to go back and read these sources more carefully and follow links within them to new research materials. It's essential to set up a system that will make it easy for you to find these materials again when you will need them.

Building a document management system

As you locate sources for your research, you need to be able to do two things: access the information you need later, when you need it, and document your sources correctly when you've completed your project (see Chapter 10). In addition, any system you come up with must be able to accommodate both online and traditional sources.

Saving information about your sources

As you locate potentially useful online sources, you need to keep track of them so you can access them later if you need to. The simplest way to track Web sources is to bookmark them in your browser (see page 29). However, a bookmark saves only the title, URL, and access date for your source. In academic research, you need to keep all of the following information (when available) about each source you use:

- Author name
- Title (of Web page, etc.)
- Title of larger work containing the source (Web site, etc.)
- Publication date
- URL
- Access date

The easiest way to store all this information is probably to save it all in a single word processing file. If your computer has enough memory, you can keep your browser program and a word processor open at the same time, using the Copy and Paste functions to move information from the Web page to your text file (see Figure 4.1). To save yourself time later, format the information according to the guidelines for your discipline. See Chapter 10 for guidelines on documentation using Columbia Online Style.

You can use a similar method to keep track of print sources, either by copying and pasting citation data from your library's electronic catalog into a text file, or using the "save as text" function from the electronic catalog, and later transferring the text into the same file as your online sources. If neither of these options is available at your library, then print or write down the citation data for the sources you use and type them into your computer file later.

Saving your source materials

Once you've saved the background information for your sources, there are two ways to save the source material itself. The first method is downloading an entire file to your computer. By choosing the Save as command from the File

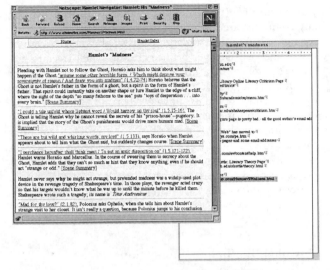

Figure 4.1: Using a word processor to track Web site
information

menu, you can save the actual text of any Web page to a
computer disk. Saving images and other media is accom-
plished by clicking and holding the mouse button on the
image (Macintosh) or clicking the right-hand mouse button
(Windows).

Downloading text files is especially useful if there is a
limit to the number of Internet-connected computers at

NETIQUETTE TIP

Printing and saving in public computer labs: Public
computer labs are a way of fairly distributing limited
resources. When printing to a networked computer,
make sure you only print the pages you need. Some
Web sites contain forty or more printed pages of text.
You can use the `Page Setup` or `Print Preview`
command to make sure you're only printing the
pages you need.

When you save files in public computer labs,
make sure you put them on your own disk, not the
computer's hard drive. Not only does this information clutter the computer, but it may be erased by
computer service personnel.

your institution. You can take these files and read them on any computer, freeing up the Internet-connected computer for research by other students. Also, since Web sites can be instantaneously changed by their creators, you'll need to preserve your source in its original form to document it for your research. It's a good idea to save the complete text of every online document you use in your research.

The second method is to print out the documents you need. Since traditional research has always relied on print sources, this can give you a sense of comfort and security as you work. But remember that whether or not a document is printed is no sure measure of reliability. Always evaluate each source you use in terms of the guidelines given in Chapter 1.

Downloading helper applications

Some Web sites require **helper applications** in order for you to use the diverse media they offer. Most commonly, you may need a helper application to view video or hear audio files, or to view specialized Web sites incorporating animation or audio. In many cases, the site itself will provide a link to a site which allows you to download the helper application free of charge. For example, the Milos Forman interview page at *http://www.hollywood.com/movietalk/celebrities/mforman/html/sound.html* requires the RealAudio helper application to listen to the interviews. To download it, you would click on the RealAudio icon, which links you to the RealAudio site at *http://www.real.com/products/player/*, and then follow the instructions posted at that site.

Generally, files you download will be **compressed**, meaning they are in a special format which must first be uncompressed with yet another helper application before they can be used. For Windows, most files can be uncompressed with WinZip, available at *http://www.winzip.com*. Macintosh files are generally compressed with Stuffit, available at *http://www.aladdinsys.com/*.

Once you've downloaded a helper application, your browser will look for helper applications in a special folder on your hard drive, usually called Plug-ins. For a complete list of plug-ins compatible with Netscape Navigator, visit *http://www.netscape.com/plugins/*.

Chapter 5

Usenet News

What are Usenet newsgroups?

Newsgroups are like public bulletin boards on the Internet—topic-specific sites of discussion and news distribution. The best thing about newsgroups is that you aren't just limited to reading messages others have posted. You can post your own message and engage other newsgroup members in conversation about an issue that interests you.

Your school will most likely be connected to **Usenet**, an enormous network of groups from around the world. The broad classification of Usenet contains thousands of topic-centered newsgroups organized hierarchically by name. The server at your school (the **news server**, or **news host**) collects and organizes the groups. You will access newsgroups with a **newsreader** (or news client), which provides an easy interface for reading, composing, posting, and downloading newsgroup messages.

Messages (or **posts**) displayed by the newsreader are varied. Many come from other Usenet users like yourself. Others may be **news feeds**, or messages posted to a newsgroup by a wire service or other traditional news source. (Note: The word *post* can be used as either a noun or a verb.) The newsgroup messages form **threads**, consisting of an original posting and a series of replies on the same topic, usually with the same subject heading. The "news" at a typical Usenet newsgroup is a mixture of multimedia, personal postings, carefully crafted articles, and conventional news feeds. The groups not only distribute these topic-centered materials, but also fulfill an important social function by providing spaces where individuals can meet and engage in discussion.

At the moment, there are more than twenty thousand newsgroups online with an estimated ten million Usenet users. Perhaps this popularity can be explained by the way that Usenet accommodates such a diversity of topics and individuals, containing groups as different as *soc.adoption .parenting*, *pets.dogs.behavior*, *alt.barney.dinosaur.die.die .die*, *misc.activism.progressive*, and *soc.culture.kurdish*.

Newsgroups can be directed at audiences ranging from the local to the international (even extraterrestrial!). Many academic institutions, for example, will offer newsgroup services for affiliated courses and individuals. Most groups, however, are global in scope. For the purposes of our discussion, we divide groups roughly into three categories: news feeds, moderated groups, and unmoderated groups.

- **News feeds** represent the most familiar form of newsgroup information. Groups based on news feeds collect traditional news from wire services like the Associated Press and Reuters. Usually listed under the large CATEGORY or "Clari" newsgroups, these groups can be extremely useful for students doing basic research, providing instant access to a wide variety of current resources. Check with your instructor about the availability of the Clari news feeds at your institution.

- **Moderated groups** operate on the premise that messages posted to the group should be filtered through a moderator; therefore, not every message sent to a moderated list will be posted. Because messages which lean toward unsubstantiated personal rants are generally censored, postings to a moderated list often fall into the category of expert opinions or topic-centered articles. Many of these posts can be well argued and offer fairly knowledgeable insight into a research topic.

- **Unmoderated groups** are open to anyone and offer the best opportunity for viewing the diverse types of written interaction that can take place on Usenet newsgroups. Messages display varying levels of formality (ranging between scholarly articles and "chat") and often prompt substantial interaction. A posted message and subsequent responses (composing a thread) reveal a dialogue that often moves between a series of arguments and counter-arguments.

Most newsgroup discussions are unmoderated and involve a range of activities and types of messages. In some ways, what you find on a newsgroup will be similar to a listserv (see pages 18–21). The postings generally relate to a single topic and often provide insight and perspectives from learned individuals that can be easily incorporated as resources for student compositions. Some newsgroups are more directly analogous to traditional print media, while others range toward personal opinion.

While individual newsgroups are limited in scope, with a substantial depth of topic in each, keep in mind that newsgroups in general are limited as a resource in other ways. While knowledgeable Internet users can provide source information for an unlimited number of issues, it may be difficult to determine if a message posted on a newsgroup is reliable. For example, a recent message on a stock-market newsgroup recommending the stock of Franklin Mutual Funds turned out to be written by the son of the company president—not exactly an unbiased source.

How to use newsgroups

Most World Wide Web browsers now incorporate newsreading interfaces that coordinate the reading and composition of newsgroup posts (see Chapter 3). To point your browser to a newsgroup, type `news:` followed by the name of the newsgroup in your browser's location box. For example, to connect to the newsgroup *alt.activism* you would type `news:alt.activism`.

Finding newsgroups on your topic

Many search engines on the Web allow you to search newsgroups. The most complete index of newsgroups is found at ***http://www.liszt.com/news/*** (see Figure 5.1 for an example of a Liszt search). Also, as you use newsgroups, you'll notice that some users post messages to more than one group. You can look at the other groups members of your group are posting to in order to find even more resources.

With literally thousands of different Usenet groups to choose from, there is an excellent chance that you will discover groups discussing issues important to you and/or useful for researching class projects. At the same time, however, the overwhelming list of groups can be disorienting, and the

Figure 5.1: Results of a Liszt search for "microsoft"

process of searching through thousands of prefixed and suffixed names can be frustrating and time consuming.

Get accustomed to the idea of browsing newsgroups as a means of gathering materials for your research papers and projects. There are a number of topics for which Usenet will offer more (and more significant) materials than a traditional library. If you use Usenet groups to research current events or topics which are frequently discussed online—Third World issues, environmental concerns, computer or technology topics—you will very likely find much more material than you would searching through a library's collection of books and periodicals.

Also remember that newsgroups offer an extremely broad array of materials. You will be able to find not only well-written articles, but also important documents (for example, government legislation or official UN statements), as well as an array of opinions and perspectives on the issue. As we suggested above, this variety of information and multiplicity of voices can be addressed through a careful process of critical reading.

Saving your research

Keep in mind that newsgroups, by their very nature, are geared toward current events. Since the groups have limited storage size, newer postings displace older ones after a certain amount of time or after the group has exceeded its size limitations. For researchers this means that the content of the groups is constantly changing, and a post that is available one week may be gone the next (especially on groups with heavy traffic). Unless you record them, resources can disappear from the group before you have a chance to get needed statistics or citation information. For this reason, always save and document any posts that you find particularly useful. If you are not sure what exactly you will need, it is always better to keep too much source information than not enough. It is a good idea to reserve a diskette solely for newsgroup resources. If you are using client software, you can archive the material you find online and "cut and paste" quotations into your papers once you have begun writing.

Posting to a newsgroup

Newsgroups closely intertwine the processes of research and conversation. You may begin using a newsgroup by gleaning information from it, but beyond just mining

---

NETIQUETTE TIP

Posting to newsgroups: Usenet focuses a tremendous amount of expertise on even the most obscure topics. Of course, the people reading and writing these groups are not librarians paid to answer questions—they participate in the discussions for their own benefit and enjoyment. Group members will resent feeling obligated to answer obvious factual or historical questions. That is why it is crucial to spend time familiarizing yourself with the key issues, terms, and players in a debate before posting questions to a group.

Be specific about what you already know on the topic, and what you need to know. Be careful with your use of important terms—the difference between "Croat" and "Croatian," for example, may be extremely important to some participants in a discussion about conflict in southeastern Europe. The best questions will spark debate on the newsgroup and allow the group members to offer assistance to the student while maintaining their existing level of conversation.

Usenet for existing resources, you should also consider posting questions and requests for information about your topic to appropriate newsgroups.

Newsgroup participants are often surprisingly helpful and may write long and thoughtful replies to student requests. In order to receive this help, though, you will need to compose your questions carefully. A confident but polite tone will go a long way toward eliciting useful feedback, but will not make up for a poorly conceived message.

Integrating newsgroups into your research

Perhaps the greatest benefit of researching with newsgroups is their immediacy. One type of group offers news feeds from wire services like the Associated Press and Reuters, providing materials that appear in newspapers around the country. News is thus available as immediately as in a newspaper or on television, with the additional strength of near comprehensive coverage: anything the wire services produce is available online, whereas any particular newspaper has to pick and choose what it has space to present.

Newsgroups often offer significant information that is absent from mainstream news sources, especially concerning international and Third World issues. For example, along with international news feeds on the uprising in Chiapas, Mexico, newsgroups have provided the text of political pamphlets from the region. Thus current, locally produced information (unfiltered by publishers) becomes available to interested readers around the world.

The "chat" groups are less useful for serious researchers. Social message boards focusing on nonacademic subjects—groups like *rec.sport.unicycling*, *rec.music.beatles*, and *alt.aliens.imprisoned*—will probably not be appropriate for your research project. Some chat groups can be useful, however. For example, the conversation on *alt.fan.tarantino* would prove interesting if your research paper considered the film *Reservoir Dogs*.

Evaluating newsgroup sources

The volume of information available on newsgroups demands evaluation and critical reading skills. Because of the comparative absence of filtering processes like those more broadly employed in print publication, excellent materials are "published" on Usenet which would otherwise find space only in low-circulation local presses, if anywhere. At the same time, because anyone with access to the Internet can post information and arguments to newsgroups, the material can often be untrustworthy.

Newsgroups are a paradox—a source of information both less reliable and more reliable than familiar items such as magazine articles. They may be less reliable because it is as easy to post (and thus "publish") off-hand messages with mistaken information as it is to post well-considered messages with viable arguments and accurate information (see Figure 5.2). Because the thoughtful and thoughtless messages appear side by side and in the same format, you need to distinguish potentially problematic messages from the two other broad categories of messages discussed above: postings from news feeds and messages from the "serious," more analytical discussion groups (which often make use of detailed research).

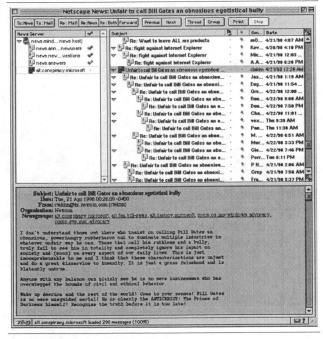

Figure 5.2: A newsgroup thread discussing Microsoft founder Bill Gates

What is significant about Usenet is that most groups make little distinction among all these various types of messages. When you read a magazine, for instance, you may notice that less "authoritative" material such as a letter to the editor is separated from the featured articles. Furthermore, you won't be able to see the many articles that were *not* selected for publication by the editors. In contrast, when you enter a thread of discussion in a newsgroup, you are instantly surrounded by a number of divergent voices and opinions, all pulling against one another in a variety of ways. If you read through this information with a critical eye, you might actually come to a fuller sense of the complexity of an issue than you might reach after reading isolated printed sources.

Chapter 6

Real-Time Discussion: IRC and MU*s

What is Internet Relay Chat (IRC)?

Internet Relay Chat (**IRC**) allows communication over the Internet as if in a conference call or over a CB radio channel. Using IRC, users can participate in topic-centered, real-time discussions over channels (or lines) that are roughly equivalent to radio frequencies.

Like the Usenet groups discussed in Chapter 5, the channels of IRC center on specific topics. In IRC channels, however, users can do more than participate on an existing channel; they can also quickly create their own channels. What makes IRC interesting is that multiple users around the globe can communicate in real time with only a slight lag between exchanges. This almost instantaneous transfer of messages in IRC allows users to communicate in a way that resembles face-to-face conversation. Unlike e-mail or newsgroups, which are **asynchronous** (i.e., there is an expected delay between messages), IRC lines allow for synchronous conversation.

This immediacy can present a problem: if your audience is not physically present, how can you convey the sorts of nonverbal signals (expressions, gestures, tone of voice, etc.) that people use in conversation? IRC allows users to send these signals with commands that represent the signal as something other than speech. Characters can use **emotes**, or descriptions of actions they are virtually "performing." For example, a user named Socrates could type `:listens intently`, and the text transmitted to other participants would read `Socrates listens intently`. In this way users can interact through writing—not only with conversational dialogue, but also by describing that dialogue.

A helpful way of looking at real-time discussions is as a hybrid that blends elements of writing and speech. A discussion in IRC reads a little like a manuscript of a play, in which a scrolling screen displays participants' names followed by a colon and then their dialogue or emotes. This sense of the theatrical is compounded by the fact that users are referred to as characters, and they often take on pseudonyms while online.

What are MU*s?

Like the IRC channels, **MU*s** offer spaces in which real-time written conversation and interaction can take place. MU* indicates a certain type of text-based, virtual environment, the first of which were the Multi User Domains (or "Dungeons"). MUDs were initially designed as a more sophisticated medium in which to engage in role-playing games like Dungeons and Dragons. Rather than use graphics to represent the fantastic worlds of these games, MUD participants could construct complex environments out of descriptive passages of text. These descriptions were placed on the Internet and scripted in a way which allowed multiple users to log on and be simultaneously present in the virtual space, adding an important interactive element to the games. Until recently these spaces have existed mainly as a forum for social interaction and gamesmanship. During the last few years, however, academics have started to see the value of these text-based environments and have begun to apply them to any number of scholarly projects.

MUDs gave birth to numerous different formats with names like MUSH and Tiny MUSH, each of which has slightly different protocols and scripting languages, as well as to the "MUD Object Oriented," or MOO. Rather than try to distinguish between MUDs, MUSHes, MOOs, and a host of other acronyms, we will use the term MU* to indicate a variety of these text-based virtual spaces. Because of the growing tendency for the more academically oriented of these spaces to be constructed using MOO scripts, we will provide examples mainly about MOO commands. Those details which do apply specifically to MOOs, however, can almost always be adapted with only minor variations to the other MU* formats.

Unlike the IRCs, the space of a MU* is a highly circumscribed environment in which the surroundings will dictate many of the user's options. Within the same MU*, a user could easily wander into and out of the reference section of a university library, a public hearing in a fourth-century BCE Grecian polis, a sci-fi nightmare, the second act of a Beckett play, the set of a movie, or just about anywhere else that someone might have imagined—all mapped out through textual descriptions. Rather than simply reading through the scrolling dialogue of an IRC channel, MU* users can move around, look at objects, and engage with their environment on a number of other levels.

MU*s and IRCs also free the class from some of the logistical constraints of the traditional classroom. A class that wanted to meet with students from another section or from another institution could log on to a MU* or an IRC environment. Similarly, an instructor could arrange to bring a number of guests from remote locations into the virtual "classroom," or send students into MU*s and IRCs that are frequented by people outside of the class itself. As we have discussed in previous chapters, this kind of interaction with an expanded audience presents an important challenge to writers. You must shape your messages for your readership and be prepared to receive engaging and sometimes challenging response and feedback.

IRC channels and online discussion

Accessing and participating in IRC is a fairly simple procedure. If you are connected directly to a Unix-based network at your institution, for example, you might simply type irc to connect to the IRC server. Often, however, you will use an IRC client program on your workstation, which provides a much easier interface for your IRC sessions. Some common IRC clients are IRCle (for Macintosh) and MIRC (for Windows). These client programs will have the locations of IRC servers—often more than a hundred—pre-scripted for easy access. If you have been given instructions to connect to a specific IRC server, you can do so easily within the IRC client program. If not, you can experiment with different servers to see the types of channels that are available on each.

Once you are connected to IRC, you will need to distinguish between commands that you issue to the IRC server and the words that you wish to communicate to the group. The first character of a command is always slash (/). Some of the basic commands allow you to list or join channels or modify your nickname. Because the IRC clients facilitate conversation, simply typing a line of text and pressing Enter will send the message to all the users currently subscribed on an IRC channel. Your nickname will be attached to the text you write so that the message will automatically be ascribed to you. Thus, after a very brief introduction to the technology, you will find that the operation of IRC discussion is, for the most part, removed to the background.

IRC commands

- `/join #rhetoric`
  Joins you to an existing channel (here, *#rhetoric*): if the channel doesn't exist, creates a new channel.
- `/list`
  Lists all currently available channels. Be aware that listing them all will tie up your machine for several minutes. Type `/help` `/list` once you are online to manage this list.
- `/nick` *newnickname*
  Changes your nickname to whatever you type in place of "newnickname."
- `/names`
  Shows nicknames of users on each channel.
- `/who` *channel*
  Shows who is on a given channel.
- `/whois` *nick*
  Shows "true" identity of someone on a channel.

To create a new IRC channel, you simply join a channel that doesn't already exist. Choose a name obscure enough that it won't already be in use, but clear enough that the people you want to participate will recognize it.

How to interact in a MU* environment

While MU*s offer a greater range of interactivity than the chat channels of IRC, they also require more time for learning the fundamentals of the medium.

As with e-mail and newsgroups, you can get to a MU* with a simple Telnet connection; this is the most basic way to connect to a server (see page 63). Enter the **IP address** followed by the port number (usually either 7777 or 8888). For example, the address of Diversity University MOO is *moo.du.org 8888*. The interface provided by this kind of connection, however, is a bit cumbersome. For instance, the other users will scroll onto the screen as you compose new messages, breaking up the text you are trying to enter.

MU*s can also be accessed by activating a client application which resides on a remote machine. Though these programs still rely on a Telnet connection, their interface allows a user to compose more easily and keep a record of the MU* session. Their operation may require knowledge of specialized commands.

Workstation client applications, such as MUDDweller or Mudling (for Macintosh) or MUTT or MudWin (for Windows), available by FTP as freeware, are the easiest way to log on to a MU*. Programs like this assist navigation, offer separate windows for composing messages, and provide easily retrievable transcripts. The simple connection and the rapid transfer of text are two reasons that MU*s have become so popular.

Many MU*s offer individual accounts to regular visitors with personalized names and passwords, and most MU*s have easy-to-use anonymous logins that allow first-time or infrequent users access to the MU*. If you plan to add any rooms or other features to the structure of a MU*, you will probably need to have an individual account on the server and permission from its system administrators.

Although some MU*s will require guests to use prefabricated identities, most will allow new users to configure temporary names and descriptions for their characters. By typing the command `@desc me as a broad-shouldered guy carrying a Frisbee`, a user named "bozo" would set his character description. Any other user who typed `look bozo` would see "a broad-shouldered guy carrying a Frisbee." You should take some time to construct a description of yourself as you wish to be seen. Define the gender of a character by typing `@gender` followed by `male`, `female`, or `neuter`; this will configure the gender of your persona with one of the traditional set of gender pronouns. You can usually see the full range of gender options on a MU* by typing `@gender` by itself. Daedalus MOO, for example, lets the user choose from a number of options: either (s/he), egotistical (I), plural (they), royal (we), splat (*e,h*), or even Spivak (e, em, eir, eirs, eirself, E, Em, Eir, Eirs, Eirself).

While we've talked about the ways that MU*s and IRCs challenge the idea of authorship through their electronic mesages, we don't want to suggest that they make a writer completely anonymous. In fact, one of the values of using IRCs, and probably to a larger extent MU*s, is that they allow students to develop alternative identities. You can experiment with online constructions of identity, as well as study audience reaction to various personas. For instance, the appearance of "an elderly, well-dressed African-American woman who would look equally comfortable lecturing in a university or serving food to the homeless with Food Not Bombs" is almost certain to change the flow of a conversation about affirmative action in institutions of higher learning.

The primary interaction that takes place on a MU* is text-based communication. The basic commands are `say` and `emote` (though these can usually be shortened to `"` and `:` respectively). The `say` command (`"`) attributes your name to any message you want to send. For example if your user name is "Athena" and you type in the line `Nobody knows you're a god on the Internet.`, everyone in the room (including you) will see the message `Athena says, "Nobody knows you're a god on the Internet."` The `say` command simply tells the MU* server to place your username and the word "says" in front of exactly what you type.

NETIQUETTE TIP

Expressing emotion in a MU*: Though all interaction is narrated in third person, you can include any number of sentences or any symbol you wish after the emote symbol. The most obvious use of this feature is to "say" things with the `emote` command. By typing a message like `:says painfully, "I didn't know that was going to happen."` you will produce `Athena says painfully, "I didn't know that was going to happen."`

Emoting allows expression of any number of different attitudes, for instance humor or irony. To express certain subtle feelings, however, you must communicate through your writing rather than through emotes.

Similarly, the `emote` command (`:`) is used to attribute actions to you. It places your name in front of the text you type after the command. For example, the line :rises   in splendor and heads for the nearest temple. will return the message Athena rises in splendor and heads for the nearest temple.

The basic MU* navigation commands are simply north, south, east, and west; but rooms in MU*s are often built to offer other dimensions of motion. A well-constructed room will inform a user about the possible options for movement and investigation. In fact, the details of a MU* environment can be quite elaborate and creative. Thus, building spaces on a MU* can require creative writing skills unlike those of the prose that may be stressed in the classroom. The well-worn dictum that descriptive writers should "show not tell" is especially pertinent for MU* environments. The skills you gain from writing precise descriptive prose for a MU* can be usefully extended to all your writing.

Basic MOO commands

Note: when you see *italic* text, replace that text with your own information.

look *object*	provides a description of the current room unless an object is specified
" *text*	allows you to "say" whatever you type in after the command
: *text*	makes your character "emote" whatever you type after the command
whisper "*text*" to *char*	speaks the message *text* only to the designated character *char*
read *name*	use to "read" newspapers or signs in MOOs
@desc me as *description*	provides a description of yourself for those who "look" at you
@gender *type*	gives your character the gender *type*
@help or help	gives more detailed information about MOO commands and their syntax
@dig "*name*"	creates a room
@desc *object* "*desc*"	describes a room or an object
@add-exit	creates an exit

@add-entrance	creates an entrance
@dig *direction* to "*room*"	links an exit and an entrance
@leave	defines what you see just before you go through an exit
@oleave	what others see when you leave
@arrive	what you see after you arrive in a room
@oarrive	what others see when you arrive in a room
@lock	prevents other users from entering a room or taking an object
@nogo	what you see if you can't go through an exit
@onogo	what others see if you can't go through an exit
@create $object type named "*name*"	creates a new object of a given type ($note, $letter, $thing, or $container)
@take	picks up an object
@take succeeded	what you see when you take
@otake succeeded	what others see when you take
@take_failed	what you see if you can't take
@otake_failed	what others see if you can't take
@drop	drops an object
@drop succeeded	what you see when you drop
@odrop succeeded	what others see when you drop
@drop_failed	what you see when you can't drop
@odrop_failed	what others see when you can't drop

Chapter 7

Other Internet Resources

Telnet

__Telnet__ is a terminal emulator: with Telnet you can establish a connection to a remote computer, almost like being at the machine's keyboard. Once connected, you can work with files in a specific portion of the computer's operating system (a __shell__), access files being shared by a server program, or activate other client programs that reside on the remote machine. You can download Telnet client applications like NCSA Telnet and Trumpet Telnet as __freeware__ from a variety of sites or sometimes obtain them directly from your institution.

You have two basic options for using a Telnet client to access information on the Internet. For example, when reading e-mail you could:

- Telnet to a shell on a mainframe and log on to the machine's mail server in order to read text files directly from the server.
- Telnet to a shell on a mainframe and activate a mailreading client that resides on that machine. This remote client program will offer the reader an improved interface for managing mail. Note, however, that this interface is still limited by the simplicity of the Telnet connection.

If the only Internet technology you have access to is Telnet, you may still be able to reach World Wide Web files. Web clients can reside on remote computers and can be ac-

cessed with a simple Telnet connection. Here, for example is
the interface for Lynx, a Unix-based text-only Web browser:

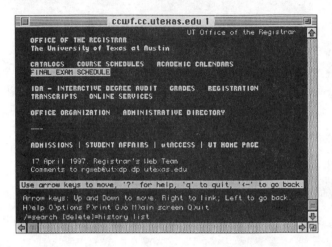

Each of the words or phrases in capital letters is a link;
links are followed using the arrow keys, and other single key-
stroke options are available. Because Web pages contain
multimedia elements, these Telnet connections give you se-
verely limited access to the Web.

File Transfer Protocol (FTP)

File Transfer Protocol (**FTP**) is a basic means by which
files—including text files, graphics, even applications themselves—are downloaded from and uploaded to central sites
by users working at their desktop computers. Transferring
files can be a difficult process (though made easier by client
programs), and we do not have the opportunity here to ex-
plain it fully. Some of the issues you will need to be con-
cerned with are: knowing the address of a site which contains
the materials you want, negotiating the directory structure
on that site, choosing the right settings for downloading the
files, and uncompressing these files to produce the resources
you desire. Your institution may maintain its own FTP site
with appropriate programs for your system.

You can find Internet client software at many FTP sites
including the following:

- *ftp.utexas.edu* (Mac only)
- *ftp.dartmouth.edu*

- *wuarchive.wustl.edu*
- *ftp.ncsa.uiuc.edu*
- *ftp.stanford.edu*

Although file transfers can be performed with programs resident on institutional servers (often by typing ftp and an address at the prompt), we strongly recommend that you look into client software for this procedure—it will alleviate many of the difficulties involved in transferring files. Most of these applications also allow you to save site addresses, login names, and directory paths as bookmarks, so you can return to especially useful sites with one click of the mouse. Two common FTP client programs are Fetch (for Macintosh systems) and Cute FTP (for Windows systems).

Because files on FTP sites are sometimes **compressed** (rewritten in a way that consumes less memory) in a variety of different formats, you will probably need to have on hand several different applications for uncompression (see Chapter 4).

You may also use FTP for uploading files to a server, as, for example, in publishing World Wide Web documents (see Chapter 8). When loading files, make sure that HTML documents and any text files are sent as **ASCII text** or **text only** and that other media are transported as "binary" or "raw data." Also make sure that file names remain unaltered during the uploading process. You may need to turn off settings on the FTP client application which append extensions to the file names. You can also use FTP to transfer large files to someone else by uploading them to an FTP site and giving them the address so they can download the files.

Gopher

Gopher was the precursor to the World Wide Web; the first truly interactive way of locating resources on the Internet. Few Gopher resources are actively maintained, but you may occasionally run across a Gopher site and you should be able to recognize it when you do. Gopher sites work nearly the same way as Web sites, and you can access them using your Web browser. Gopher sites will appear in results of Web searches on the major search engines. URLs for Gopher sites are preceded by the protocol *gopher://*

```
Gopher://gopher2.tc.umn.edu/
```

Chapter 8

Publishing Your Own Documents on the World Wide Web

Many people approach **HTML** (**Hypertext Markup Language**) as if it is some horribly arcane and mysterious computer code that is only decipherable by a few gifted hackers. Believe it or not, publishing Web pages is really quite easy—and learning HTML is the easiest part of learning to publish effective Web sites.

One way to think about HTML is as a complicated typewriter. You can't produce a good essay, story, or report without knowing how to use the typewriter, but learning to use the typewriter doesn't necessarily mean you can write great poetry.

One of the things that makes HTML different from a typewriter is that as soon as you've produced your poem, essay, slide show, guidebook, or whatever, it's instantly available to anyone in the world with access to the World Wide Web—literally millions of people. This immense size of the Web's audience is also probably the most important thing to keep in mind as you create your Web site. Your audience is the global community of users of the Web, so your Web document should be easy to use for that audience—not the much more limited audience consisting of your classmates and instructor. Put yourself in the shoes of someone who hasn't taken your class, read the books you have, or even used the same kind of computer you're using. Your Web site should be accessible to them, as well as to your local audience.

There are six fundamental components of creating a good Web site. You'll notice that the actual HTML coding is just one of the six components. Most industry insiders believe it's much more difficult to find someone proficient at the "content development" phases—planning, authoring, and designing—than the "technical" phases—coding and posting.

The six components of Web site creation
  1. Planning
  2. Authoring
  3. Designing
  4. Coding
  5. Posting
  6. Publicizing

Planning a Web site

Most great writers are extremely well read. By the same principle, most good Web site designers have spent a lot of time surfing the Web, both to get ideas for their own sites and to learn from the mistakes others have made.

As you prepare to create your own Web site, spend at least an hour or two surfing the Web looking at sites similar to the one you're planning. If you've done research on the Web, go back to some of the sites you liked. As you surf, don't just pay attention to the content of a site—consider how easy it is to navigate. Can you find the information you're looking for, or do you have to spend extra time seeking it out? When you need to visit a different portion of the site, are navigational buttons easy to find and understand, or do you have to scroll a long distance to the top or bottom of the page? Do pages load quickly, or do you have to wait for huge image or sound files to download? Are graphic images used appropriately, or do they distract from the overall message of the page?

If you make a list of the features of good Web sites versus bad ones, you'll begin to see how much thought and advance planning must have gone into the good sites. Among the most important considerations are:

  • How will the information on my site be organized?
  • How much information should appear on each Web page?
  • How will visitors navigate from page to page and around the site?

- What information should be presented graphically? As text? Should any other media be used? Audio? Video? Animation?
- How much memory is available for the site?
- What will the site's URL be?

Structuring your Web site

Deciding on an organizing principle may be the most difficult decision you make as you plan your site. Unfortunately, it's also one of the first decisions you'll need to make. Preparing an outline of the material you want to cover should help. Also, look at Figure 8.1, which gives three common organizational structures for Web sites. You should not feel constrained by these structures, but all have been used to create effective Web sites. One of the advantages of hypertext over traditional media is that it allows you to follow a nonlinear organization for your document. However, be aware that visitors to your site can easily become confused if you do not provide a logical and easy to follow structure.

If you can't decide on one organization for your site, you can create alternate structures. For example, if you choose the hierarchical organization in Figure 8.1, you can also place a "next" link on each page that allows the visitor to read the pages in sequence: 1, 2a, 3a, 3b, 2b, 3c, and so on. Most visitors will expect to find a **home page** somewhere on your site, from which it is easy to navigate to any of the other pages on your site.

NETIQUETTE TIP

Structuring your Web site: Make sure the structure of your site is readily apparent to visitors. Make it difficult for visitors to get "lost" in your site by providing a link to a site directory on each page.

Once you've decided on an organizing principle, you'll need to determine how much material to include on each page. As you surfed the Web, you probably got some idea of the range of sizes for a single Web page. Some pages contain the equivalent of forty or more printed pages. Some contain just a single word. While any size in between can be appropriate, remember the constraints your users are operating under. While your

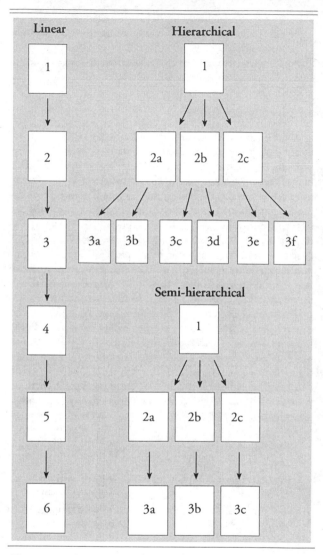

Figure 8.1: Common Web site organizational structures

university may have a high-speed connection to the Internet, most users are connecting over regular phone lines at speeds substantially slower. Just one small image may take up to a minute to download. While that may not seem long, consider the thousands of other options your visitors have access to. Sixty seconds is the length of two full-length television commercials. Is your Web site as exciting as Air Jordan and the Energizer Bunny combined? A good rule of thumb is that a single Web page should take no more than fifteen seconds to download over regular phone lines. That's two or three pages of text, plus one or two small, memory-optimized graphics.

Presenting information on the Web

The Web allows you to present information in the form of text, images, and even sound, video, and animation. Text can be in tables, paragraphs, or even flying across the screen. Images can be photos, charts, and graphs designed for ornamentation or information. As you consider how to present information, remember that each method has advantages and limitations. Some of these are summarized in Table 8.1. The table is arranged according to increasing memory requirements. It's also important to note that each medium requires specialized software to produce. Though text and image-editing software is relatively abundant, software for animation, audio, and video can be quite expensive.

Type	Advantages	Limitations
Text (TXT)	Uses least memory. Easily printed and saved.	In a graphics-oriented environment, some visitors may lose interest.
Images (GIF, JPEG)	Uses moderate memory. Stable on many different types of computers.	Can be overused. Can take a lot of time to prepare.
Animation (GIF)	Uses moderate memory. Useful when well done.	Can be annoying. Usually in poor taste.
Audio (WAV, AU)	Only way to present certain types of data.	Uses substantial memory. Can be very annoying. No Internet-wide standard for file format.
Video (AVI, MOV, MPG)	Only way to present certain types of data.	Uses most memory. No Internet-wide standard for file format. Very slow on almost any platform.

Table 8.1: Advantages and limitations of different information types

The media you choose will, of course, depend on your topic. If your Web site analyzes the songs of various birds, for example, then audio will be an essential component. However, if it considers only the poetry of Mary Wroth, then text will likely be the most important medium for your site.

Since text is the "cheapest" in terms of computer memory and time it takes to create, most Web sites contain a lot of text. But if the purpose of a site is to display a collection of photos or original artwork, for example, a lot of text may simply get in the way of the message you're trying to convey. Whatever medium you choose for your Web site, make sure you've made an informed decision.

Authoring your site

Once you've made the important decisions about what information you will present on your site and how it will be presented, the next step in the process is authoring. **Authoring** is an awkward word, but it is probably the most descriptive term for the process of creating the content material that will be presented on a Web site. Authoring is roughly analogous to writing the manuscript for a book, the script for a play, or taking the photos for a public exhibition. As a content author, you create or obtain from other sources all of the information that will be presented on your site.

Crucial to the process of authoring a Web site is considering the experience that visitors to your site will have when they visit. David Siegel, author of *Creating Killer Web Sites*, suggests that the experience of visiting a site should be like going to a restaurant, where visitors first see an enticing entrance, which leads them to a host, who guides them to a table, where they are presented with a tempting menu of choices to select from (Figure 8.2). In contrast, Jim Rhodes of Deadlock Design feels a Web site is more like a place for one-on-one conversation. Since visitors are typically sitting by themselves in front of a lonely computer screen, Rhodes contends, a Web site should talk to them like a close friend—chatty, casual, with lots of inside information (Figure 8.3).

Clearly, many different approaches to Web authoring have been successful; however, all successful site authors carefully consider the experience of the visitor as they create content (Figure 8.4). What might your potential visitor be looking for? What is the clearest, easiest, and most efficient way to give it to them? What information will visitors bring with them? Are there any existing Web sites that provide back-

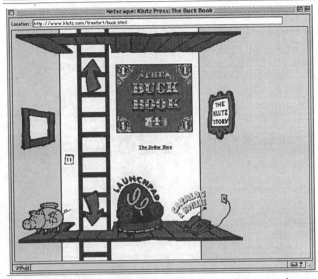

Figure 8.2: Many Web authors like to create a complete atmosphere, much like a themed restaurant.

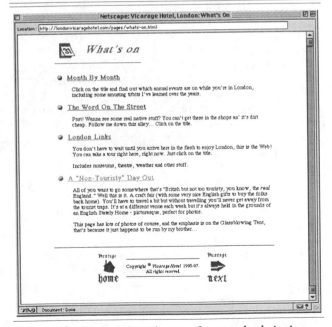

Figure 8.3: Some Web authors prefer to style their sites after a conversation between close friends.

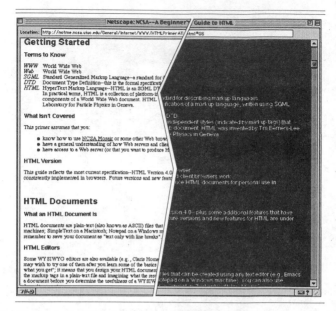

Figure 8.4: The two faces of a Web site. Depending on
how visitors set their browsers, the same Web
site can appear very different.

ground information that might be useful to your visitors?
What tone and style will be most useful and appealing for
your visitors—formal? casual? irreverent? Are people clamor-
ing for the information your site will provide or is the information unavailable elsewhere? If so, they might be willing to
tolerate long downloads for your information. If not, you'll
need to impress them with high-quality writing, crisp images,
and quick downloads.

Content authoring clearly requires proficiency in whatever medium you're producing: writing for text, artistic ability for images, musical ability for sounds. It also requires
varying degrees of computer skill, depending on the
medium. While writing is an art form that may take years to
master, the only technical skill you need to produce text for
a Web site is the ability to operate a word processor. In addition to artistic talent, creating images for the Web requires
the mastery of one or more **image editors**. An image editor
is a computer program designed to create and modify images. The most common image editor for Web applications
is Adobe Photoshop. However, almost every program that
can create an image can save it in a Web-compatible format.

Ultimately, you'll need to create a **GIF** or a **JPEG** image, so make sure whatever image editor you use supports one or preferably both formats. If you're planning on using photos on your Web site, you'll either need access to a **scanner** to convert the photo into a computer file, or you'll need to use a commercial film processor that offers **Photo CD** service.

Guidelines for writing on the Web

Writing on the Web is different from any other form of writing. While printed documents almost universally have a clear beginning, middle, and end, Web sites are accessed in a variety of sequences and contexts, even framed by other sites. Visitors to your site can and often do easily skip on to the relevant portion of your site—or to another site, if they don't find what they're looking for at yours. Keep to the following guidelines unless you have a good reason:

- Since users may enter your site on any page, make sure each page can stand on its own. Help your readers by offering a link to a site map or home page for your site.
- Write in simple, direct sentences that get right to the point.
- Speak directly to your reader: address them as "you," rather than "all of you" or "he or she." Remember, your audience may be thousands of people, but each one of them is generally visiting your site alone with his or her computer.
- Keep paragraphs short—reading long paragraphs on-screen can be tiring.
- Break up your writing with heads and subheads.

--- **NETIQUETTE TIP** ---

Linking to other Web sites: Links give the Web tremendous power because they allow users instant access to other relevant resources. When you link your site to another, as a courtesy you should let the author of that site know you're linking. Make sure you give credit to the authors of sites you link to—don't make it appear as if someone else's work is actually your own. If you display these common courtesies when you create your site, you may be rewarded as well: others will link to your site, and your work will become part of a truly worldwide community.

- Try to limit each page on your site to no more than one or two screens of information.
- Work Internet links into the context of your writing. Remember that the user doesn't need to see the entire URL of the site you link to—just enough information to identify the site.

Guidelines for creating images on the Web

While it's beyond the scope of this text to discuss the technical aspects of image creation, we can offer a few pointers:

- Keep images as small as possible. Most users have small monitors: 640 by 480 **pixels** is most common.
- Use as few colors as possible. The more colors, the more memory your image uses.
- When possible, use **Web-safe colors** (see page 94).
- Only include relevant images. Since images take time to download, make sure they are relevant to your discussion.
- On the other hand, don't skimp on images. Users will quickly tire of page after page of text.
- Make sure you have permission to use borrowed images. Remember, copyrighted images cannot be placed on the Web without permission. If you can't get permission to use a graphic that's already on the Web, you can always include a link to the existing Web site.

Designing your site

Once you've created the content that will appear on your site, you're ready to design the site itself. Perhaps the easiest way to do this is simply to sketch it out with pencil and paper. What will visitors see when they arrive at your site? A table of contents? Introductory text? A tone-setting photo? Where will visitors click to get to the main content pages of your site? Will each page include navigational links users can click on to access the main parts of your site, or will visitors be forced to visit each page in sequence? What will your headings look like? Where on each page will images appear? Now is the time to decide on the details of how your site will unfold to visitors.

The way you make these design decisions is up to you. You may use pencil and paper, as described above. If you're like Web design master David Siegel, you could create a layout of each page on your site using Adobe Photoshop. Or you can use your word processor's formatting capabilities to generate the basic look and feel of your site.

Once you've made these critical decisions, you're ready to take the final step before actually posting your site on the Web: coding in HTML.

HTML: The language of the Web

How do you create a file that is publishable on the Web? There are two methods: coding in HTML and using a **Web authoring system**. See page 99 for more on authoring systems. The rest of this section will focus on coding in HTML.

Take the text you've created in any word processor, save it as "text only", name it text.html, and open it with a Web browser. Most browsers will read simple text only files and display them the same way any Web page is displayed.

Figure 8.5 shows the results of saving a raw text file and opening it with a Web browser. The first thing you'll notice is that your text's all there, but the formatting is gone. Your title is not centered, paragraphs aren't indented—in fact, the whole thing is one big paragraph. That's the first lesson to learn about HTML—your browser will strip away all the formatting you use in your word processor and replace it with plain, unformatted text. Don't worry, there's a way to add this formatting back to your document. In fact, HTML allows you to do much more than that. Throughout this section, we'll gradually build a small Web page starting from a simple text file. When you're done, you'll be able to build a similar Web page yourself.

Figure 8.6 shows the same file with a few basic formatting commands added. As you can see, adding the formatting commands has made our text file look much worse, but it has made the actual document visitors will see much more attractive. In HTML, all the formatting commands are called **elements**, which in turn are made up of **tags** enclosed in angle brackets. By examining the example shown here, you can notice a few things about HTML tags:

- All tags must be enclosed in angle brackets.
- Though it's not required, tags are easier to locate in your HTML file if you type them in ALL CAPS.

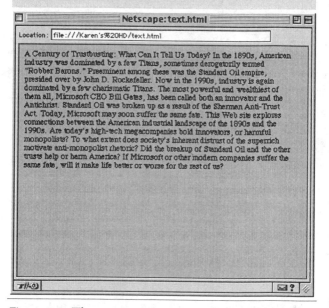

A Century of Trustbusting:
What Can It Tell Us Today?

In the 1890s, American industry was dominated by a few Titans, sometimes derogatorily termed "Robber Barons." Preeminent among these was the Standard Oil empire, presided over by John D. Rockefeller.

Now in the 1990s, industry is again dominated by a few charismatic Titans. The most powerful and wealthiest of them all, Microsoft CEO Bill Gates, has been called both an innovator and the Antichrist.

Standard Oil was broken up as a result of the Sherman Anti-Trust Act. Today, Microsoft may soon suffer the same fate.

This Web site explores connections between the American industrial landscape of the 1890s and the 1990s. Are today's high-tech megacompanies bold innovators,

Netscape: text.html

Location: file:///Karen's%20HD/text.html

A Century of Trustbusting: What Can It Tell Us Today? In the 1890s, American industry was dominated by a few Titans, sometimes derogatorily termed "Robber Barons." Preeminent among these was the Standard Oil empire, presided over by John D. Rockefeller. Now in the 1990s, industry is again dominated by a few charismatic Titans. The most powerful and wealthiest of them all, Microsoft CEO Bill Gates, has been called both an innovator and the Antichrist. Standard Oil was broken up as a result of the Sherman Anti-Trust Act. Today, Microsoft may soon suffer the same fate. This Web site explores connections between the American industrial landscape of the 1890s and the 1990s. Are today's high-tech megacompanies bold innovators, or harmful monopolists? To what extent does society's inherent distrust of the superrich motivate anti-monopolist rhetoric? Did the breakup of Standard Oil and the other trusts help or harm America? If Microsoft or other modern companies suffer the same fate, will it make life better or worse for the rest of us?

Figure 8.5: The text you type in a word processor and the same text displayed on a Web browser

```
<H1 ALIGN="Center">A Century of
Trustbusting</H1>
<H2 ALIGN="Center">What Can It Tell Us
Today?</H2>

In the 1890s, American industry was
dominated by a few Titans, sometimes
derogatorily termed "Robber Barons."
Preeminent among these was the <B>Standard
Oil</B> empire, presided over by <B>John
D. Rockefeller</B>.<P>
Now in the 1990s, industry is again
dominated by a few charismatic Titans. The
most powerful and wealthiest of them all,
<B>Microsoft</B> CEO <B>Bill Gates</B>,
has been called both an innovator and the
Antichrist.<P>
Standard Oil was broken up as a result of
the <B>Sherman Anti-Trust Act</B>. Today,
Microsoft may soon suffer the same
fate.<P>
```

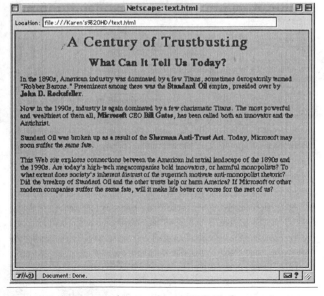

Figure 8.6: Text with some basic HTML formatting
displayed on a browser

- Most elements require an opening tag (for example <B> for bold text) and a closing tag to signal the end of that element (in this case, </B>). All closing tags start with the slash character (/). The most important elements that don't require closing tags are <P> (paragraph),
 (new line), <HR> (horizontal rule), and <IMG> (image).

- Some tags take **attributes**, which give additional information about how the tag is to be applied. For example, here the <H1> tag also includes the attribute ALIGN="Center". This combination tells the browser to not only display the text as a first-level heading, but also to center that text.

In this example, we created two levels of centered headings using the <H1> and <H2> tags combined with the ALIGN="Center" attribute. You can specify up to six levels of headings (<H1> through <H6>, but hopefully you'll never need more than three), and you can also specify Left, Right, and Justify with the ALIGN attribute.

We also placed several important terms in boldface type using the bold tag, <B>. You can also create italic (<I> . . . </I>), underlined (<U> . . . </U>), and larger or smaller type (<BIG> . . . </BIG>, <SMALL> . . . </SMALL>).

Paragraphs are specified in HTML using the <P> tag. Most browsers will place an extra line of space between each paragraph. If you don't like this look, use the <BR> tag to take you to a new line with no space.

Adding structure, links, and images

You now know how to make a passable Web page using HTML. However, this page still has a few flaws. First, it doesn't contain any links to the rest of the Web, or even to other pages on this site. It's rather uninteresting visually, with a dull gray background and no images at all.

In Figure 8.7, many of these problems have been addressed. The document has now been structured as a formal HTML file. The HTML structure tags are <HTML>, <HEAD>, and <BODY>. <HTML> and </HTML> tags should surround the entire document. Then the document should be split into two parts, the Head and the Body.

The Head contains descriptive information about the HTML document. In this case, the only information is the Title tag, which causes the title to appear in the browser window framing the document. If you don't include a Title tag, the name in the browser window becomes simply the file name (see Figure 8.7).

The Body tag surrounds the rest of the file and can have several attributes. In this case, we've specified white as the background color, green as the link color, red as the color for links the visitor has already visited (VLINK), and black as the text color. In addition, you can specify a background image to be displayed behind all text and images in the document. What you can't see in the figure is that the file name has also been changed to *index.html.* This is the standard file name for home pages. The benefit of using *index.html* as your file name is that you don't have to type it in the location box to point your browser to the file. Just type the domain name and any subdirectories, and your browser will automatically open *index.html.*

Links

One of the most powerful features of HTML is the ease with which documents from all over the world can be linked together. The standard format for an HTML link is:

```
<A HREF=URL>Hot Text</A>
```

In this case, you'd substitute in the URL of the document users will see when they click on "Hot Text." In Figure 8.7, "John D. Rockefeller" is hot, and when visitors click on that text, they will be transported to a biography of Rockefeller at *http://voteview.gsia.cmu.edu/entrejdr.htm.* Several links have been added to our sample Web site. Look closely at them to see how they work. Note that the links at the bottom of the page link to **local** files. In this case, the link only requires the file name, and that's all you should provide. That way, while you're coding your Web site, you can keep all the files on your own local workstation. When you're finished coding, you can post your site to the server, and assuming you keep all your files in the same directory, all the links will still work. If you had used absolute references (see page 87) when building your site, they wouldn't work after the files were uploaded.

Images

We've added a banner headline to our document instead of relying on the <H1> tag to provide formatting. This sort of simple artwork can add a bit of flair to a page. Many site designers use image files not only for document headlines, but also for subheadings, to assure a uniform look on different users' systems. If we could have obtained permission, we

```
<HTML>
<HEAD>
<TITLE>A Century of Trustbusting</TITLE>
</HEAD>
<BODY BGCOLOR="White" LINK="Green"
VLINK="Red" ALINK="Red" TEXT="Black">
<IMG SRC="banner.gif" HEIGHT="119"
WIDTH="500" ALT="A Century of Trustbusting:
What Can It Tell Us Today?">
<P>
<HR>
<P>
In the 1890s, American industry was
dominated by a few Titans, sometimes
derogatorily termed "Robber Barons."
Preeminent among these was the <B>Standard
Oil</B> empire, presided over by
<A HREF="http://voteview.gsia.cum.edu/
entrejdr.htm">John D. Rockefeller</A>.<P>

Now in the 1990s, industry is again
dominated by a few charismatic Titans. The
most powerful and wealthiest of them all,
<A HREF="http://www.microsoft.com/
presspass/">Microsoft</A> CEO
<A HREF="http://www.vanderbilt.edu/Owen/
froeb/mgt352/MrBill.html">Bill Gates</A>,
has been called both an innovator and the
Antichrist.<P>

Standard Oil was broken up as a result of
the <A HREF="http://k7moa.gsia.cmu.edu/
antitrst.htm">Sherman Anti-Trust Act</A>.
Today, Microsoft may soon suffer the same
fate.<P>
This Web site explores connections between
the American industrial landscape of the
1890s and the 1990s. Are today's high-tech
megacompanies bold innovators or harmful
monopolists? To what extent does society's
inherent distrust of the superrich motivate
anti-monopolist rhetoric? Did the breakup
of Standard Oil and the other trusts help
```

```
or harm America? If Microsoft or other
modern companies suffer the same fate, will
it make life better or worse for the rest
of us?<P>

<P ALIGN="Center"><A
HREF="standard.html">The Standard Oil
case</A> - <A HREF="social.html">Social
reactions to billionaires</A><br> <A
HREF="mscase.html">Microsoft antitrust
case</A> - <A HREF="outlook.html">The
outlook for the future</P>
</BODY>
</HTML>
```

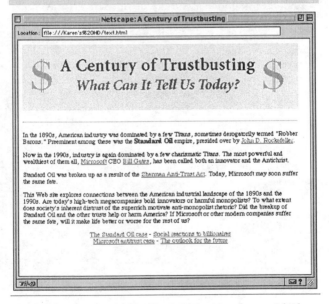

Figure 8.7: A complete HTML Web page along with the
text file required to generate it. Note especially
how the <A> tag is used to create hot text.

also probably would have included photos of Bill Gates and
John D. Rockefeller, to personalize the page even more. Here
is the general format for placing an image in a document:

```
<IMG SRC="imagename.gif" HEIGHT=pixels
```

```
WIDTH=pixels ALT="Text appearing if user can't
see the image">
```

Look at Figure 8.7 to see how the words in *italics* get modified for a specific image. Note that in order for your browser to recognize a file as an image, the file name should always end in *.jpg* or *.gif* to indicate the type of file it is (see pages 85–87 for a discussion on how to prepare images for the Web). In almost every case, the HEIGHT and WIDTH you specify should be the same as the actual dimensions of the image file you created. Otherwise, the image will look distorted and ugly. The ALT text is especially important because many users do not have graphical monitors, and others with slow Internet connections will turn the images off on their browsers. It also provides the only information of any kind blind visitors will get (unless your site includes audio files).

Another important attribute of the <IMG> tag is ALIGN. Note that ALIGN works differently for images than it does for the <P> and <H1> tags. With images, the ALIGN attribute specifies how the text in the document will wrap around the image. "Left" and "Right" are the most valuable, because they allow the accompanying text to wrap around the image, as in Figure 8.8. You can also specify "Top", "Bottom", and "Middle", but these are of limited use because they only place one line of text next to the image.

You cannot use the ALIGN attribute to center an image horizontally on the page. The only way to accomplish this is by surrounding the <IMG> tag with a <P> . . . </P> tag, as follows:

```
<P ALIGN="Center"><IMG SRC="imagename.gif"
Height="pixels" WIDTH="pixels" ALT="Centered
Image"></P>
```

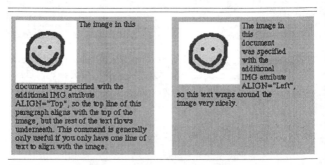

Figure 8.8 Results of different applications of the ALIGN attribute for images

Considerations while you're coding

As you code your Web page in HTML, it's easy to check your code to see if it's working. Just remember to save your HTML file as text, and include the extension `.html`. Then you can open the file in your browser and see what it looks like as you work. If you know you've made a change in the text file, but it doesn't appear in your browser, just click on `Reload` and the page will be updated to include your new coding.

It's probably a good idea to keep both your browser and text editor open while you work, so you can easily go back and forth between the two and correct mistakes as they come up.

Preparing images for the Web

The key to making memory-efficient image files is understanding how computers save memory. The two major file formats save memory in two different ways: very basically, <u>**GIF**</u> files (pronounced "jiff") save memory by limiting the number of colors in a document, while <u>**JPEG**</u> files (pronounced "jaypeg") save memory by limiting the resolution of a document. Depending on the particular image, either format can produce more savings. Again speaking very generally, GIF files work better for line drawings or typographical art

---

NETIQUETTE TIP

Images on the Web: Images are what separate the professional Web designer from the millions of casual Web users who've managed to post their own Web pages. You can spot a novice Web designer in a minute by simply observing how efficiently he or she's used images. A 148K image on a home page is a sure sign of someone who doesn't know what he or she's doing. Experts know how to use memory more efficiently, so even large images take up less than 20K. (A <u>**kilobyte**</u>, usually abbreviated <u>**K**</u>, is simply a unit of measure of memory for computer files—on the Web, smaller is better.) A 148K file might take over a minute to download over slow phone lines. By that time, your visitor has probably surfed on to a site in Tanzania.

---

consisting of one to twenty distinct colors. JPEG files work better for continuous tone images like photographs or paintings with lots of details and thirty or more distinct colors.

While it's beyond the scope of this book to give specific instructions on creating images, the following should help you optimize your images for the Web once you've created them. Our instructions are based on Adobe Photoshop 4.0, but most image-editing programs have similar commands. For more on creating images for the Web, consult *Photoshop for the Web* by Mikkel Aaland (Cambridge: O'Reilly, 1998).

Optimizing GIF files

When you create an image from scratch, create it using a "Web palette"—usually an option in most image-editing programs. Make sure you create it at the actual size you'll be using on your Web page. Remember that most users have 640×480 monitors, so you certainly won't want to specify an image size larger than this. Then export it to **GIF89a** format as described below.

If you're adapting an image someone else created, make sure it's in Color RGB format. You can specify this by selecting RGB Color from the Mode menu in Photoshop. Then make your image the size you want it to appear on your Web page (in pixels) using the Image Size command on the Image menu. Write down the dimensions of your image in pixels—you'll need this when coding your HTML.

What comes next is the key to optimizing your file. You're going to change your file format from RGB to Indexed Color. With Indexed Color, you can specify the number of colors your document uses. The fewer colors, the less memory your image consumes. With many images, you can get the number of colors down to less than ten with no significant loss of resolution. Try it. Just select Indexed Color from the Mode menu, select Adaptive Color, type the number of colors you want, and press OK. Start with a small number, like 10. If the result looks great, you may be able to do better. Select Undo from the Edit menu and try a smaller number. Repeat these steps until you find the smallest number of colors that produces an acceptable image. You may get even better results if you select a Web palette first.

To export the file, select GIF89a from Export on the File menu. Type a file name ending in .gif. Make sure you write down the file name so you have access to it while you're coding.

Optimizing JPEG files

Optimizing JPEG files is done in a similar way. Once you've made your image the size you want, choose Save As from the File menu. Type a new name ending in .jpg and select JPEG as the file format. You can then choose from four different image quality settings. The lower the image quality, the less memory the image consumes. Even the lowest setting produces surprisingly good results. You can then look back at your image and decide if the loss of resolution is acceptable. It's important to save your original image file as well as the JPEG file in case you want to edit the file later or you decide to change the resolution.

If you need to include a very large (over 50K), detailed image on your Web site, you should consider making two images—a small (3–4K) placeholder image and the full-size original image. You can code your HTML so that when users click on the small image, the larger image is downloaded onto their browser:

```
<A HREF=largeimage.jpg><IMG SRC=smallimage.jpg
HEIGHT=pixels WIDTH=pixels ALIGN="Left">Click to
download a larger image</A>
```

File management while coding

As you code your Web site, you will begin to generate a considerable number of files. The most important rule of Web file management is to keep only files destined for your Web site in the directory containing your HTML and image files. Any files such as non-HTML word processing files, non-GIF or JPEG image editor files, or other data you may have used to create your Web site should be kept separate from your Web files.

If the number of distinct files required for your site exceeds thirty, you may want to consider adding a directory structure to your site. For example, if you have a hierarchical site with four major subdivisions, you may want to create a subdirectory for each of the subdivisions, each placed inside the main directory (which contains only the files for your home page).

Relative vs. absolute URLs

Once you reorganize your site to include subdirectories, the way you link to pages on your own site must change.

When linking to an outside Web site, you always need to use the complete URL (the **absolute URL**). However, when linking to a file located in a subdirectory of your own site, you should use the local or **relative URL**. This is a partial URL that takes advantage of the fact that your browser already "knows" the URL of the current Web page. The simplest relative URL is one you're already familiar with—just using the name of the file for URLs in the same directory. To link to a file in a subdirectory of the directory you're in, use the following syntax:

```
<A HREF="subdirectoryname/file.html">hot text</A>
```

Once you're in a subdirectory, getting back to your site's main directory without resorting to absolute URLs requires another bit of syntax. The notation ../ means "the directory containing the current directory" and can be used to go "backward" in the current directory tree. Thus, if your file is in a subdirectory, and you'd like to link back to the main page in the directory containing it, use this syntax:

```
<A HREF="../index.html">hot text</A>
```

DON'T use

```
<A HREF="parentdirectoryname/index.html">hot
text</A>
```
(this syntax will NEVER work)

Because keeping track of relative references can be difficult, many professional Web designers keep all their files in the same directory even if the total number of files exeeds one or two *hundred*. At some point, however, you'll simply have to subdivide, so learning relative notation is essential for proper file management.

Posting your site to the Web

After you've constructed your site to work perfectly on your local computer, it's time to post it to your institution's Web server. Up until now, you've been the only person with access to your site. Posting your site on the server means that everyone in the world with access to the Web can see your site.

What the server does

Serving files involves two major activities: 1) overseeing the behind-the-scenes operations of the Web server, including setting up form and imagemap routines, and running software which provides the proper protocol for sharing files on the Web; and 2) managing directory structures and files which reside on the Web server. Organizing your files and uploading them to a server may require some extra time and energy, especially if you are uncomfortable with the various technologies. Whatever your level of technological knowledge, we recommend that you coordinate with your Web administrators as you work through the various tasks involved in serving your files.

Usually your computer services center or some other institutional entity will be responsible for the operations of the Web server, so you will probably not be involved in the first of these two activities (if you do need information about the server-side operations of the Web, see *http://Web66.coled.umn.edu/Cookbook/*). Some institutions will provide students with individual accounts for Web building, but in many cases, the instructor will be responsible for managing files for the entire class.

Uploading files

There are two main ways to upload your files to your server. If your computer is connected directly to your campus network (for example, a Windows NT network), you may be able to copy your files directly to the server the same way you do locally. Otherwise, you'll probably be using FTP (see Chapter 7). You may be able to load all of your directories at once, depending upon your FTP software. Otherwise, you will need to place files on the sever individually. In any case, check that the final organization of the directories and files that you load to the server mirrors the structure of any projects developed locally. Additionally, when loading files, send HTML documents and any text files as ASCII text or text only and other media as binary or raw data. Make sure that file names remain unaltered during the uploading process. Finally, after you have placed files on the server, you should check the links with a browser to ensure that nothing has gone wrong.

Publicizing your site

Once you've posted your site, you want people to visit it, right? Otherwise, you might as well have left it on your local computer. Fortunately, there are many free and easy options for publicizing your site on the Internet. The simplest is to post a brief message describing your site (including its URL, of course) on relevant newsgroups (see Chapter 5) and list-servs (see Chapter 2).

Next, you may want to try to get your site indexed on the major Web search engines and indexes. Most search engines have an "Add URL" feature that allows you to type your site's URL and a brief description that will appear when your site is listed in someone's search. In addition, you should specify the keywords you'd like your site to be listed under in your page's actual HTML file. You do this using the <META> tag, which goes in the <HEAD> section of your file. For example, the Trustbusters page might utilize Meta tags like this:

```
<HEAD>
<TITLE>A Century of Trustbusting</TITLE>
<META KEYWORDS="Antitrust, Microsoft, Bill
Gates, Standard Oil, John D. Rockefeller,
trustbusters, Sherman Anti-Trust Act, Social
Attitudes">
<META DESCRIPTION="An analysis of the effect of
and attitudes toward trustbusting and the
Microsoft Antitrust case">
</HEAD>
```

Publicizing Web sites has become an industry in itself. There are many sites devoted to Web site promotion, but the best is probably Jim Rhodes's The Art of Web Site Promotion at *http://www.deadlock.com/promote/*.

Advanced HTML techniques

Imagemaps and graphical links

One way to maximize the organizational potential of a Web site is to incorporate the use of **imagemaps** into its layout. An imagemap is a graphic image that has been "mapped" by HTML commands so that clicking on different portions of it will link the user to different sites or files, most often to different areas of a Web site. The author configures hot spots on the image, and a reader who clicks on one of the hot spots will be sent to whatever link has been assigned to that spot.

Imagemaps can be useful, as they provide a visual navigational tool for the site. We should caution that not all servers support imagemaps, and configuring the hot spots and links is somewhat sophisticated. Check with your server administrator before deciding to use imagemaps (for more information about making imagemaps, see *http://www.webcom.com /html/tutor/imagemaps.shtml*).

You do not need to use an imagemap to add graphical links to your Web site. By placing an image in a Web page and then creating a link from that image, you can design a site that uses visual elements to facilitate a reader's movement without having to learn the complex operation of imagemaps. Use small images to make links, and make sure the images convey a sense of the link to be followed; a small picture of a house, for example, could be used to indicate a return link to your home page.

Using forms to interact with a Web audience

A **form** is a mechanism by which Web browsers allow users to send information back to the server. If at all possible, include a comment form with each of your Web projects. Most comment forms are configured to send e-mail to the author of a Web page. Here is a sample comment form.

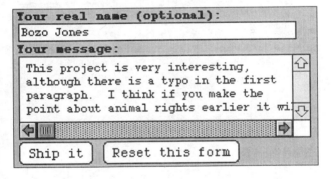

By using interactive comment forms, you can engage the Web's global audience. As with imagemaps, the ability to use interactive forms will depend upon the capacities of your Web server. Check with your server administrator about using forms. Many browsers now support the <MAILTO> HTML command, which can be configured to send e-mail to an author. If your server does not support forms, you should consider including a <MAILTO> option in your pages to facilitate contact. While the sample above shows the most basic contact form, you can modify forms to include fields

for other information. (For more on forms, see *http://www
.yahoo.com/Computers_and_Internet/Internet/World_Wide
_Web/Programming/Forms/*).

A guide to HTML commands

Headings

```
<H1> . . . </H1>  largest heading
<H2> . . . </H2>
<H3> . . . </H3>
<H4> . . . </H4>
<H5> . . . </H5>
<H6> . . . </H6>  smallest heading
```

Font styles

`<B> . . . </B>`	**Bold-face text**
`<I> . . . </I>`	*Italicized text*
`<U> . . . </U>`	<u>Underlined text</u>
`<TT> . . . </TT>`	`Typewriter font`
`<STRIKE> . . . </STRIKE>`	~~Strike-through text~~
`<SUP> . . . </SUP>`	Superscript text
`<SUB> . . . </SUB>`	Subscript text
`<BIG> . . . </BIG>`	Large font
`<SMALL> . . . </SMALL>`	Small font
`<CENTER> . . . </CENTER>`	Centered material

Lists and menus

Definition list

```
<DL>
<DT>E-mail
<DD>The basic form
   of Internet com-
   munication.
<DT>Emote
<DD>Virtually rep-
   resents an ac-
   tion during
   real-time conver-
   sations on IRCs
   and MOOs.
</DL>
```

E-mail
   The basic form of Internet communication.
Emote
   Virtually represents an action during real-time conversations on IRCs and MOOs.

Unnumbered list

```
<UL>
<LI>Milk
<LI>Bread
</UL>
```

- Milk
- Bread

Numbered list

```
<OL>
<LI>Milk
<LI>Bread
</OL>
```

1. Milk
2. Bread

Menu Lists

```
Heading
<MENU>
<LI>Milk
<LI>Bread
</MENU>
```

Heading
Milk
Bread

Links

The most common is the link to a document or file:

```
<A HREF="URL/file name"> . . . </A>
```

You can also make a link to a target within a document. Begin by placing a target anchor in the desired spot in the document.

```
<A NAME="target name">
```

Next, make a link to the target by using the # sign and specifying the target name in the link information.

```
<A HREF="#target name"> . . . </A>
```

You can also link to a sound, graphic, or video file by specifying the proper file name in the link information.

	Links to:
`<A HREF="URL/filename.gif">...</A>`	gif image
`<A HREF="URL/filename.jpg">...</A>`	jpeg image
`<A HREF="URL/filename.mpg">...</A>`	mpeg movie
`<A HREF="URL/filename.mov">...</A>`	Quicktime movie
`<A HREF="URL/filename.au">...</A>`	sound file
`<A HREF ="URL/filename.wav">...</A>`	sound file

Inline images

Inline images are graphics which are incorporated into the layout of a Web page. To place an inline image in a document, select the point in the document where the image should appear and use the command:

```
<IMG ALIGN=bottom SRC="imagefilename.gif">
<IMG ALIGN=middle SRC="imagefilename.gif">
<IMG ALIGN=top SRC="imagefilename.gif">
<IMG ALIGN=left SRC="imagefilename.gif">
<IMG ALIGN=right SRC="imagefilename.gif">
```

Background attribute

The background attribute allows the user to specify an image file to use as a background for the Web page. This attribute is applied to the body element, discussed above. For example, at the beginning of the body section of a Web page, the element `<BODY BACKGROUND="imagename.gif">` tiles the window background with the designated GIF image. When the background attribute is utilized, the end tag to the body section is still simply `</BODY>`.

Colors

Recently, the use of color on Web pages has expanded widely and is supported by most Web browsers. Colors can be given to a number of page elements. You can specify the most basic colors: `"White"`, `"Red"`, `"Green"`, etc. by just typing their names. In HTML, strict colors are designated by six-character codes representing their relative red/green/blue (RGB) values. Because of the complexity of these codes, you may want to use an HTML editor which supports the application of color. In such an editor, a shade is selected from a color wheel and the corresponding RGB values are placed automatically in the HTML script.

Also, you might refer to one of the many Web sites that provides the codes for the 216 Web-safe colors that display correctly on both Macintosh and Windows platforms (for example, *http://www.lightsphere.com/colors/*).

Colors are specified by using a hexadecimal value for each component of the color: red, green, and blue. Two digits are allowed for each component, specified in the order red, green, blue. The lowest possible value for a color is 00; the highest value is FF. Hence, solid red would be FF0000, solid green would be 00FF00, solid black would be 000000, and solid white would be

FFFFFF. You can specify millions of colors using these codes, but it is recommended you select from the 216 standard colors.

Colors are usually applied as attributes to the <BODY> element, and should be specified in the opening tag. If one of the following attributes is used, they should all be specified in order to avoid color conflicts. If, for example, a visitor to your page has set the Web browser to display text in the same color you gave to your background, this would make the page unreadable.

<BODY BGCOLOR="#*rrggbb*">	sets the background color for the page as a whole
<BODY TEXT="#*rrggbb*">	sets the text color for the page as a whole
<BODY LINK="#*rrggbb*">	sets the unvisited link color for the page as a whole
<BODY VLINK="#*rrggbb*">	sets the visited link color for the page as a whole
<BODY ALINK="#*rrggbb*">	sets the activated link color for the page as a whole

All these attributes should be specified in a single <BODY> tag, like so:

```
<BODY BGCOLOR="#FFFFFF" TEXT="#000000"
LINK="#FF0000" VLINK="#00FF00" ALINK="#00FF00">
```

Colors may also be applied to selected text within the body of a Web page. The element <FONT COLOR="#*rrggbb*"> . . . </FONT> will set the color of the text between the tags to the designated shade.

Tables

HTML tables are contained within <TABLE> . . . </TABLE> tags. The fundamental elements of an HTML table are <CAPTION>, which defines a caption for the table, and <TR>, which defines a table row. Each row in turn contains cells, either for a header, defined by <TH>, or for data, defined by <TD>. (Although in this example we are using only numerical data, text and even graphic files can be entered in a data cell as well.) Each cell should be closed with the appropriate ending tag, either </TH> or </TD>.

The caption may be aligned to the top, bottom, left, or right of the table by adding an ALIGN attribute to the <CAPTION> tag.

By default, a table is flush with the left margin, but it can be centered by placing the entire table script within <CENTER> . . . </CENTER> tags. Additionally, a BORDER attribute may be added to the <TABLE> tag, which indicates that the table should be drawn with a border around it and between each of the table's cells. Adding a value (in number of pixels) sets the outer border of the table to the specified width.

To combine all these features, you can create a table using the following script:

```
<TABLE>
<CAPTION ALIGN="bottom">Academy Award Winning
African American Actors</Caption>
<TR><TH>Actor</TH><TH>Movie</TH>
<TH>Year</TH></TR>
<TR><TD>Whoopi Goldberg</TD><TD><I>Ghost</I>
</TD><TD>1991</TD></TR>
<TR><TD>Cuba Gooding Jr.</TD><TD><I>Jerry
Maguire</I></TD><TD>1997</TD></TR>
<TR><TD>Louis Gosset Jr.</TD><TD><I>An Officer
and a Gentleman</I></TD><TD>1983</TD></TR>
<TR><TD>Hattie McDaniel</TD><TD><I>Gone with the
Wind</I></TD><TD>1940</TD></TR>
<TR><TD>Sidney Poitier</TD><TD><I>Lilies of the
Field</I></TD><TD>1964</TD></TR>
<TR><TD>Denzel Washington</TD><TD><I>Glory</I>
</TD><TD>1990</TD></TR>
</TABLE>
```

The resulting table would be displayed as:

Actor	Movie	Year
Whoopi Goldberg	*Ghost*	1991
Cuba Gooding Jr.	*Jerry Maguire*	1997
Louis Gosset Jr.	*An Officer and a Gentleman*	1983
Hattie McDaniel	*Gone with the Wind*	1940
Sidney Poitier	*Lilies of the Field*	1964
Denzel Washington	*Glory*	1990

Academy Award Winning African American Actors

You can also experiment with adding the CELLPADDING= and CELLSPACING= attributes to the <TABLE> element, which dictate (in number of pixels) the amount of space surrounding the contents of cells and the width of the borders between cells, respectively. More complex tables are clearly illustrated on the Netscape Web site, at ***http://www.netscape.com/assist/net_sites/table_assist.html***. With their more advanced features, HTML tables can provide not simply a way to present data clearly, but a strategy for Web page design itself.

We can take our simple table above to the next level by using more detailed and specific commands. Note that this level of precision requires much more code for what some would consider to be only an incremental improvement.

```
<BODY BGCOLOR="WHITE">
<TABLE CELLPADDING="0" CELLSPACING="0"
WIDTH="350">
<CAPTION ALIGN="bottom" WIDTH="350"><FONT
COLOR="Blue">Academy Award Winning African
American Actors</FONT></CAPTION>
<TR>
   <TD COLSPAN="3" WIDTH="350"><HR></TD>
</TR>
<TR>
   <TD HEIGHT="16" WIDTH="125"
   ALIGN="Left"><FONT
   COLOR="Red"><B>Actor</B></FONT></TD>
   <TD HEIGHT="16" WIDTH="175"
   ALIGN="Left"><FONT
   COLOR="Red"><B>Movie</B></FONT></TD>
   <TD HEIGHT="16" WIDTH="50" ALIGN="Left"><FONT
   COLOR="Red"><B>Year</B></FONT></TD>
</TR>
<TR>
   <TD COLSPAN="3" WIDTH="350"><HR></TD>
</TR>
<TR>
   <TD HEIGHT="16" WIDTH="125"
   ALIGN="Left">Whoopi Goldberg</TD>
   <TD HEIGHT="16" WIDTH="175"
   ALIGN="Left"><I>Ghost</I></TD>
   <TD HEIGHT="16" WIDTH="50"
   ALIGN="Left">1991</TD>
</TR>
<TR>
   <TD HEIGHT="16" WIDTH="125" ALIGN="Left">Cuba
   Gooding Jr.</TD>
   <TD HEIGHT="16" WIDTH="175"
   ALIGN="Left"><I>Jerry Maguire</I></TD>
   <TD HEIGHT="16" WIDTH="50"
   ALIGN="Left">1997</TD>
</TR>
<TR>
```

```
   <TD HEIGHT="16"  WIDTH="125"
   ALIGN="Left">Louis Gosset Jr.</TD>
   <TD HEIGHT="16" WIDTH="175"
   ALIGN="Left"><I>An Officer and a
   Gentleman</I></TD>
   <TD HEIGHT="16" WIDTH="50"
   ALIGN="Left">1983</TD>
</TR>
<TR>
   <TD HEIGHT="16" WIDTH="125"
   ALIGN="Left">Hattie McDaniel</TD>
   <TD HEIGHT="16" WIDTH="175"
   ALIGN="Left"><I>Gone with the Wind</I></TD>
   <TD HEIGHT="16" WIDTH="50"
   ALIGN="Left">1940</TD>
</TR>
<TR>
   <TD HEIGHT="16" WIDTH="125"
   ALIGN="Left">Sidney Poitier</TD>
   <TD HEIGHT="16" WIDTH="175"
   ALIGN="Left"><I>Lilies of the Field</I></TD>
   <TD HEIGHT="16" WIDTH="50"
   ALIGN="Left">1964</TD>
</TR>
<TR>
   <TD HEIGHT="16" WIDTH="125"
   ALIGN="Left">Denzel Washington</TD><TD
   HEIGHT="16" WIDTH="175"
   ALIGN="Left"><I>Glory</I></TD>
   <TD HEIGHT="16" WIDTH="50"
   ALIGN="Left">1990</TD>
</TR>
<TR>
   <TD COLSPAN="3" WIDTH="350"><HR></TD>
</TR>
</TABLE>
</BODY>
```

This code produces the following table:

Actor	Movie	Year
Whoopi Goldberg	*Ghost*	1991
Cuba Gooding Jr.	*Jerry Maguire*	1997
Louis Gosset Jr.	*An Officer and a Gentleman*	1983
Hattie McDaniel	*Gone with the Wind*	1940
Sidney Poitier	*Lilies of the Field*	1964
Denzel Washington	*Glory*	1990

Academy Award Winning African American Actors

Note that the specification of a width and height for each table cell allows precise control over the positioning of each element in the table. We used the COLSPAN attribute to generate horizontal rules extending all the way across the table.

You can use tables to position graphics and text as precisely as if you were laying them out on paper. For example, you could use a table to place a directory of your site in column form along the left-hand side of the page, and then create a second column for text. Tables are also used to create the effect of "margins," which are otherwise difficult to create in HTML. Simply make a three-column table with a single   (non-breaking space) character in each of the two outside columns, and run your text down the middle.

When you're using tables and other high-level tricks to give your page a particular look, make sure you test them on both Netscape and Microsoft browsers to verify that all visitors to your site have the same experience.

If you're interested in using tables to give very fine control of the look of your entire Web site, visit David Siegel's Creating Killer Web Sites at *http://www.killersites.com/tutorial/index.html*.

Using Web authoring systems

While **Web authoring systems** allow you to create Web sites without an understanding of HTML, it's still best to view them as time- and labor-savers rather than as foolproof systems for novices to create Web sites. With a good authoring system, you can:

- Instantly see how your page will look as you create it. For example, you could move an image around on the page to determine where it would look best, or experiment with different color schemes to see which you like best.
- Calculate download times to see how long it will take the typical user to view your page.
- Automate the posting of your site to the Web.
- Interactively manage your entire Web site. For example, you could open several pages on your site simultaneously and easily interlink them.
- Make global changes to your site without repeating them on each page. For example, if you wanted to change the background image on each page, some au-

thoring systems allow you to specify that this change will be implemented throughout your site.

Becoming an HTML expert

Believe it or not, most HTML experts didn't get that way by reading a lot of books about it. Books have their place, but the best way to learn the tricks of the trade is to see how others have done the kinds of things you'd like to do. Because HTML documents are designed to be viewed on a variety of platforms, their source HTML code is available to anyone who knows where to look. The best HTML programmers learned their trade by looking at what others have done and then combining that knowledge with their own creative energy.

When you're visiting any Web page, you can look at the source code for that page simply by selecting the View Source command from the File menu. The raw HTML for that page will appear—usually in a helper application.

If you look carefully at the HTML tags for the page, you'll soon learn how the designer created the page. You can use the same strategy in your own HTML code. Take care, however, when you use someone else's ideas. Learning how to use HTML by looking at someone else's source code is all right, but copying someone's words, images, or design can be a violation of copyright laws. See the Appendix for a discussion of copyright law and the Internet.

For more information about HTML commands, visit the Introduction to HTML and URLs site at *http://www.utoronto.ca/webdocs/HTMLdocs/NewHTML/intro.html*.

Chapter 9

Giving Credit to Your Sources: Copyright Online

There are two reasons you should give proper credit to your sources:

1. You can get in a lot of legal trouble if you don't.
2. You can get in a lot of academic trouble if you don't.

Almost any work you find on the Internet is protected by copyright. The author of a work has the sole power to determine its use and distribution. It is illegal to reproduce this work in almost any form unless the copyright holder gives you permission. This chapter covers the legal issues surrounding using someone else's ideas in your work. Chapter 10 covers the academic issues in giving credit to your sources.

Here are some situations where copyright issues affect your research and writing online:

1. You download a photograph from a commercial, subscription-based Web exhibition and include it in your Art History paper.
2. You want to post your essay on Gwendolyn Brooks's poem "We Real Cool" on the class Web site. In your essay, you quote the entire poem—eight lines, which you typed in by hand from your textbook, taking care to credit the author of the poem.
3. Someone e-mails you a speech by Kurt Vonnegut. You post it to a national Vonnegut Listserv, giving proper

credit in MLA form to the speech's author, Kurt Vonnegut, and obtaining permission from the person who e-mailed you the speech.

4. You find a joke posted on a Usenet newsgroup. The joke contains no copyright notice, so you post it on your personal Web page.

5. You publish a scathing critique of Stephen King's latest novel in both the print and online versions of your school newspaper, quoting the entire first paragraph and discussing its failings in detail, pointing to specific examples throughout the book and revealing the plot twist at the book's climax. You obtain no permission from the author or the publisher of the book.

When you reproduce a copyrighted work without the permission of the copyright holder, in most cases, you are violating the law. There are two important exceptions to the law, illustrated in examples 1 and 5 above.

Make single copies of copyrighted work for educational use

You may reproduce a copyrighted work for your personal educational use, as in a paper submitted only to your instructor or discussed in class (assuming you give proper credit to the author, as discussed in Chapter 10). This is the "educational use" provision of the law.

Make many copies of copyrighted work or publish on the Web if it meets fair use guidelines

You may also publish extracts from a copyrighted work if you're publishing a critical analysis or review of the work. You may not reproduce the entire work, however, and you must give credit to the original source. While applications of the law vary, as a rule of thumb, never quote more than 300 words or 10 percent of a work, whichever is less. As long as your comments are not libelous, copyright law protects your right to print extremely negative criticism of copyrighted works without permission. This is the "fair use" provision of the law.

Find out if a work is copyrighted before you reproduce it

Never assume a work is not copyrighted, even if you see no copyright notice. Copyright law does not require a notice—any original work you produce is protected by copyright laws unless you explicitly give permission to reproduce it. Here are two cases when it is acceptable to reprint a work that is not your own without obtaining permission (but you must still give credit to your source):

1. The copyright has expired. In the United States, you can be fairly certain a work's copyright has expired seventy-five years after it was first published. In Great Britain and much of the rest of the world, copyrights expire fifty years after the death of the author. (The U.S. law has now been revised to match the rest of the world, but it will be at least forty years before copyrights under the new law begin to expire.)
2. The author has given a blanket permission to use the work or placed the work in the public domain.

Determining whether the copyright has expired may take some research. Make sure you have determined the most recent revision date of the work you're using. For example, Strunk's *The Elements of Style* was first published in 1909; its copyright has expired and you are free to reproduce that version of the text. However, E.B. White's revision of the text remains copyrighted; you cannot reproduce that work without permission.

Some Web sites offer free graphics and sounds that you may download and use on your own Web page. If you use such images, make sure you comply with any terms of usage posted on the originating site.

Many government documents such as the *Congressional Record* are in the public domain. Be careful, however—even the *Congressional Record* may contain copyrighted material quoted from other sources. When in doubt, request permission.

Request permission to reproduce copyrighted work

If you make a document available to the public, you must get permission to reproduce any copyrighted material it con-

	Critical Analysis
Paper turned in to instructor	A
Paper posted to class listserv	A
Posting to national listserv	300/10
Newsgroup posting	300/10
Web site	300/10

A: Always okay
E: Educational materials only

**Table 9.1: Use this table to determine when you
need to request permission to reproduce a copyrighted**

tains. Refer to Table 9.1 to determine whether you need to request permission to reproduce copyrighted material in your document.

Locating the copyright holder

To obtain permission to reproduce the work, you must first determine who holds the copyright. If you're quoting from a source on the Web, look for a copyright statement, usually found at the bottom of the Web page. Often an e-mail link will be provided, and you can e-mail the copyright holder directly. Otherwise, you may need to e-mail the Webmaster for the site to find out who to contact.

If the work you want to reprint comes from a book, the copyright statement is generally found on the page following the book's title page. The copyright holder is generally the author or the publisher, but it might be someone else entirely. Make sure the portion of the book you want to reproduce has not been reprinted from some other work. If it has, you'll probably need to locate the original source to find all the information you need. Even if the author holds the copyright for the work, the best course of action is usually to contact the publisher. Try visiting the publisher's Web site and searching for "permissions department." Many publishers

Critical Reviews	Summary or Paraphrase	Complete or Partial Work	Illustration
A	A	A	A
A	A	E	E
300/10	E	N	N
300/10	E	N	N
300/10	E	N	N

N: Never okay

300/10: Okay to reproduce 300 words or 10 percent, whichever is less

work in your context. In each case, you must give credit to the author.

now provide electronic links for requesting permissions. For other publications such as newspapers and magazines, you follow a similar procedure.

Sending the letter of request

To request permission to reproduce a work, send a polite letter or e-mail explaining how and where you wish to use the work. Explaining that you are a student and that you only intend to use the work for educational purposes will go a long way. Often this process takes several weeks and may result in permissions fees, so you probably want to have a backup plan in case you do not receive permission to reproduce the work you want.

After you receive permission to reproduce a copyrighted work, it is essential that you give the rights holders credit as they specify; otherwise you may still be in violation of copyright law. In addition, you must give proper academic credit to your sources as specified in Chapter 10.

Chapter 10

Giving Credit to Your Sources: Documenting Online Sources

Any time you use someone else's words, images, sounds, or ideas in your academic work, you must give them proper academic credit. Even if you simply "forget" to give credit to your sources, you can fail a class or even be expelled from school for **plagiarism.** You should be aware that if your instructors suspect you of cheating, they can use the powerful tools of the Internet to check your work. Simply by entering a suspicious phrase from your essay into a search engine, an instructor can quickly discover if your work is truly your own.

The most important reason to document your sources is to help others learn from your work. Even if your paper is only read by your instructor, you may have found an idea that your instructor wants to follow up on—the result of your instructor's efforts could be a published book, journal article, or Web site with credit given both to you and to the sources you cite in your paper. If you publish your work on the Web, you could be helping thousands of others learn from your work, and by directing them to the sources for your work, you can help them learn even more.

Determine how sources are documented for your type of project

Because research and learning can take many different forms, each discipline has its own rules for how to document sources. For example, scholars in the Humanities are often interested in the actual written words, so the author and page number are given in MLA citations. Social scientists are often more interested in how recently a study was conducted, so the author and date are given in APA citations. Your instructor might specify additional rules or guidelines based on the needs of your class. Be sure to check on your course syllabus or with your instructor to determine the proper method for documenting sources in each class.

Using the Columbia Online Style to document electronic sources

It is beyond the scope of this book to give guidelines for documenting every type of source in every discipline. However, many disciplines have not yet published usable guidelines for citing electronic sources, so here we offer a brief summary of the **Columbia Online Style** (COS for short). COS was developed by Janice R. Walker and Todd Taylor to address some of the shortcomings of MLA and APA documentation styles. Be sure to get your instructor's permission before you use COS to document sources. For more information about COS, visit the COS Web site at *http://www.columbia.edu/cu/cup/cgos/*, or consult *The Columbia Guide to Online Style* by Janice R. Walker and Todd Taylor (New York: Columbia University Press, 1998).

Documenting sources usually consists of three steps:

1. Collect information about your source.
2. Format the documentation according to COS guidelines.
3. Integrate the source material into your project.

Documentation is easiest if you collect the required information when you locate your source. It may be difficult or even impossible to retrace your steps if you need to get additional information later. The remainder of this chapter will show you how to document online sources using the COS–MLA format. Though we do offer a general APA example, if you need to use COS–Scientific style format, you should visit the COS Web site or consult the printed version of the guide.

Collecting information about your source

COS documentation requires six basic pieces of information about each source you cite:

- Author
- Title of work
- Title of larger work containing the work
- Publication date
- Electronic address
- Date of access

Sometimes not all of this information is given for your source. Make an effort to collect all available documentation information when you first locate the source. To save time later, you may want to go further and format the reference for each source into COS style as soon as you locate it. If your computer has enough memory, keep your word processor and a Web browser open at the same time while you are researching. You can avoid errors if you make a habit of copying and pasting each source's documentation information directly from the source into a text file.

Formatting the documentation according to COS–Humanities guidelines

List each source you use on a separate "Works Cited" page and arrange them alphabetically by author (or title, if no author name is provided). Follow the general format below.

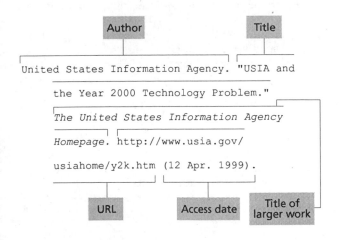

COS Documentation Examples. Though it is important to understand the general format of COS style, it can also be helpful to see how this format is applied to specific examples. When you locate a source, match the type of source you find to the examples below. For example, if you locate a Web site which gives a date for the last time it was updated, then you would format your documentation like example number 2: Web Site, Revised.

1. Web site

```
Tada, Yuriko. "Intelligible Differences: On
    Deliberate Strategy and the Exploration
    of Possibility in Economic Life."
    Professor Charles F. Sable. 1997.
    http://www.columbia.edu/~cfs11/
    IntelDif.html (12 Apr. 1999).
```

2. Web site, revised

Replace the publication date with the revision date.

```
Martin, Dave. "Honors Requirements." Davidson
    College: Department of Economics. Rev. 26
    Jan. 1999. http://www.davidson.edu/
    academic/economics/honors.html.
    (12 Apr. 1999).
```

3. Web site with institutional/group/corporate author

Replace the author name with the publishing institution.

```
American Institute of Indian Studies (AIIS).
    "South Asia Art Archive: Kanchi: Slide
    3373." Center for Electronic Text and
    Image. Rev 7 Apr. 1998. http://www.library
    .upenn.edu/etext/sasia/aiis/architecture/
    kanchi/3373.html. (12 Apr. 1999).
```

4. Web site with no author or sponsoring institution

```
"Invasion of the Big Apple." German UFO
    Watch. http://aircooledmind.org/
    alien3.html/ (12 Apr. 1999).
```

5. Web site maintained by an individual

Use the abbreviation "maint." to indicate an individual who simply collects links or other material but does not significantly contribute to the content on a site.

```
LeMar, Jason, et. al., maint. "Indiana
    Academy Science Events." The Indiana
    Academy for Science, Mathematics, and
    Humanities. http://www.bsu.edu/
    teachers/academy/scievents.html.
    (12 Apr. 1999).
```

6. Web site—Government

For regularly updated sites, give only the access date.

```
United States Information Agency. "USIA and
    the Year 2000 Technology Problem." The
    United States Information Agency
    Homepage. http://www.usia.gov/usiahome/
    y2k.htm. (12 Apr. 1999).
```

7. Web site—Book available in print and online

Give information on both the printed text and online version when available.

```
Shakespeare, William. As You Like It. 1600.
    Ed. Alan Brissenden. Oxford: Oxford UP,
    1994. http://www-tech.mit.edu/
    Shakespeare/Comedy/asyoulikeit/
    asyoulikeit.html (16 Apr. 1999).
```

8. Web site—Online article

```
Roulston, Christine. "Separating the
    Inseparable: Female Friendship and Its
    Discontents in Eighteenth-Century France."
    Eighteenth Century Studies. 32:2 (1999).
    http://muse.jhu.edu/journals/
    eighteenth-century_studies/v032/32
    .2roulston.html (14 Apr. 1999).
```

9. Web site—News service/online newspaper article

If no author's name is given, list the name of the news service. Otherwise, cite as an online article.

```
Associated Press. "India's Government
    Resigns." USA Today. http://www.usatoday
    .com/news/world/nwssat01.htm (18 Apr.
    1999).
```

10. Web site—Article from an archive

Cite as you would a printed article, but list the name of the archive site ("Archives" in this case) before the URL.

```
Rosenberg, Yuval. "Fox Fights Parkinson's."
    Newsweek. 30 Nov. 1998. "Archives."
    http://newsweek.washingtonpost.com/nw-srw/
    issue/22_98b/tnw/today/nm/nm01we_1.htm
    (16 Apr. 1999).
```

11. Web site—With frames

Some Web sites are programmed to divide your browser window into several smaller windows called **frames**. Depending on how the frames have been programmed, the URL displayed in your browser may not correspond to the actual URL of the particular frame you are referencing. Cite as you would an unframed Web page, but list the URL of the main frames page, followed by the instructions for getting to the page you are referencing.

```
Strapex AG. "Industries."  Rev. 27 Oct.
    1996. Strapex. http://www.strapex.com/
    Industries (21 Apr. 1999).
```

12. Web site—Image, audio, or video file

You may list the URL of the source file or the Web page on which it appears. If no separate title of the resource is given, list the file name.

```
Aui-Yonah, Yael. "The World of Creation."
    http://www.art.net/TheGallery/vision/
    yael2.htm (16 Apr. 1999).
```

13. Personal e-mail

Do not give the author's e-mail address.

```
Shepard, Mary. "Graduation." Personal e-mail
    (13 Apr. 1999).
```

14. Listserv

Include the address of the list. Do not give the author's e-mail address.

```
Seabrook, Richard H. C. "Community and
    Progress." cybermind@jefferson.village
    .virginia.edu (22 Jan. 1994).
```

15. Newsgroup

Give the author's name or alias, the subject of the message, posting date, the newsgroup URL, and date of access.

```
ctakim. "Unfair to Call Bill Gates an
    Obnoxious Egotistical Bully." 21 Apr.
    1998. news:alt.conspiracy.microsoft
    (19 Apr. 1999).
```

16. Gopher or FTP site

```
Greenpeace. "Greenpeace Tours North Oil Rigs
    on Brett Spar Anniversary." Greenpeace
    Campaign Archive. 1996. Gopher://gopher
    .greenpeace.org:70/00/campaigns/oceans/
    1996/jun20 (16 Apr. 1999).
```

17. Telnet site

Include any steps necessary to access the relevant information after the telnet address, separated by a single space.

```
"Experimental Nuclear Reaction Date
    Retrieval Program." National Nuclear Data
    Center. telnet://bnlnd2.dnc.bnl.gov
    (16 Apr. 1999).
```

18. Synchronous communication

Give the name (if known) or alias of the speaker, the type of communication (e.g., personal interview), and the address.

```
Pine_Guest. Personal interview.
   Telnet://world.sensemedia.net 1234
   (12 Dec. 1994).
```

19. Online encyclopedia article

List by author (if available), and give the online service you used to access the article (if not accessed via the World Wide Web).

```
"Roland (de La Platiere), Jeanne-Marie."
   Encyclopedia Britannica Online.
   http://www.eb.com:180/bol/
   topic?eu=85963&sctn=1 (16 Apr. 1999).
```

20. Online dictionary article

List by the word you looked up and give the online service you used to access the article (if not accessed via the World Wide Web).

```
"Slag." WWWebster Dictionary. Merriam-Webster
   Online, 1999. http://www.m-w.com/cgi-bin/
   dictionary (16 Apr. 1999).
```

21. Material from a CD-ROM

List author (if available) and title. Include version number and copyright date.

```
"Women's Suffrage Multimedia Map." The
   Grolier Multimedia Encyclopedia. Vers.
   7.0.4. Danbury, CT: Grolier, 1995.
```

22. Software

```
Microsoft Word. Vers. 98. Redmond, WA:
   Microsoft, 1998.
```

─── NETIQUETTE TIP ───

Linking to online sources: If you publish your project on the Web, format the "Works Cited" section as links (see page 81) to sources available online. Link the in-text reference to the full citation and format the URL of the source as hot text linking to the actual resource. As a courtesy, be sure to ask your sources for permission to link to them. Some Web sites give blanket permission to link; in this case it is still appropriate to notify the Webmaster that you have linked to the site so they can alert you if the URL changes.

Integrating the source material into your project

When you begin creating your project, whether it's a research paper, oral presentation, poster, or Web site, you need to make sure you give credit to your sources each time you use information from them. In most cases, this is done with a parenthetical reference to the author and page number, like this:

```
The Grateful Dead didn't mind people taping
their concerts, but didn't want to see people
selling the tapes for profit (Barlow).
```

However, since most documents on the Internet don't have "pages" like books or journals, the page number can be omitted.

If you work the author's name into the text itself, you don't need a parenthetical reference at all for Internet sources (for print sources, you would always need to add the page number in parentheses).

```
Grateful Dead member John Perry Barlow points
out that the band didn't mind people taping
their concerts as long as they didn't sell the
tapes for a profit.
```

Try to make parenthetical references as inconspicuous as possible—the point is to give your readers an opportunity to refer to your source, not to intrude into the flow of your project.

If the work you cite has no author, substitute the title in quotation marks, or an abbreviated version of the title if the title is long.

Brief guidelines for using COS–Scientific style

The main difference between the COS–Humanities style and the COS–Scientific style is that in most scientific disciplines, scholars place more importance on the date of the work cited, while in the humanities, the actual words written or spoken are seen as more important. "Works Cited" are called "References" in the scientific style, and the date of the work comes immediately after the author name in the reference list.

List each source you use on a separate "References" page and arrange them alphabetically by author (or title, if no author name is provided). Follow the general format below. For more specific guidelines, consult *The Columbia Guide to Online Style.*

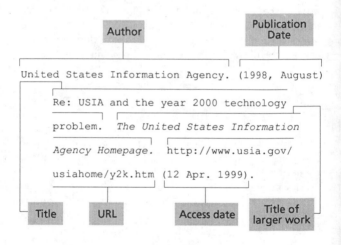

When you integrate the source material into your project, make sure you reference both the author (or title) and date of the work:

```
The Grateful Dead didn't mind people taping
their concerts, but didn't want to see people
selling the tapes for profit (Barlow 1998).
```

Chapter 11

A Case Study: Researching Literature on the Internet

Researching literature on the Internet poses some unique challenges. Writing has traditionally required only a pen or pencil and paper, and it has taken a while for the literary community to catch up with the high-tech world. Also, because the literary community is often painfully aware of the complexities of copyright law, it has shown some reluctance to place literary works and works of criticism on the Internet. And because "publishing" has always been the primary goal for "serious" poets, dramatists, writers, and critics, the Internet may have suffered, because publishing a work there isn't generally considered to be the same as "real" publishing.

With those concerns in mind, the Internet can provide tremendous resources for literature researchers. These resources tend to be the most comprehensive in two areas—works like Shakespeare's plays or the poems of Elizabeth Barret Browning, whose copyrights have expired; and "nontraditional" literature such as cowboy poetry, which has often been excluded from the mainstream press. There is also a considerable amount of biographical information on individual authors. Popular authors like Kurt Vonnegut may even have several fan pages. Newsgroups and listservs offer up-to-the-minute conversations on current issues in literature and criticism. Finally, the Internet has made the libraries of the world accessible to everyone—provided you allow enough time to request their materials via interlibrary loan. The rest of this chapter will take a step-by-step approach, following a student, Cindy Jones, as she completes her research project.

Step 1: Identify your topic

Cindy is taking Introduction to Literature and was assigned a major research paper on "an important theme in a work covered in this class." The assignment requires that she draw on at least ten outside sources and give a close textual analysis of the work. Cindy has decided to write a paper on William Shakespeare.

Step 2: Narrow the focus of your topic and begin to formulate your thesis

One good way find information to help narrow your topic is to browse with a Web subject directory. (For more on Web subject directories, see page 30. Cindy chooses Yahoo! at *http://www.yahoo.com/* and begins to click on directory topics. She clicks on progressively narrower topics: Arts and Literature, Humanities, Genres, Drama, Playwrights, William Shakespeare. There she finds dozens of sites which focus on the Bard (see Figure 11.1). After visiting several of the sites and reading some commentary, she narrows her topic:

```
William Shakespeare
Hamlet and William Shakespeare
Madness in Hamlet
The Method in Hamlet's Madness
```

As Cindy works, she makes note of the sites she may want to revisit later.

When you're brainstorming for a topic, you could also try looking through the past postings in a newsgroup (see step 4)—it might give you an idea for your paper just by seeing what other people are talking about. For example, the Shakespeare newsgroup (*humanities.lit.authors. shakespeare*) has discussed such topics as which *Hamlet* movie is the best, the true authorship of Shakespeare's plays, and even some humorous inferences based on Shakespeare's works.

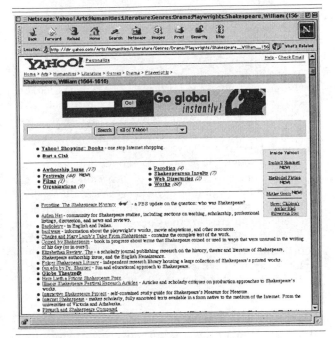

Figure 11.1: The "Shakespeare" subject directory in
Yahoo!

Step 3: Create a research plan

Cindy makes a new folder on her computer's hard drive
entitled "Shakespeare Project." She also makes a new bookmarks folder on her computer's Web browser for the topic
(for more on bookmarks, see page 29). Cindy has decided to
keep track of her sources in a text file on her computer. For
more on managing Web research, see Chapter 4.

Step 4: Investigate and join
newsgroups and listservs

Newsgroups (see Chapter 5) and listservs (see Chapter 2)
give you a chance to observe and participate in ongoing discussions about your research topic. It's a good idea to observe
and join these groups early in the research process so you get
a sense of how they can help you. Cindy goes to the Liszt

search engine at ***http://www.liszt.com*** and searches for list-servs using the keyword "shakespeare" (Figure 11.2). Cindy decides to join SHAKESPER: The Global Electronic Shakespeare Conference, which has over 1,500 members.

Cindy also locates the ***humanities.lit.authors.shakespeare*** newsgroup and notes the URL in her bookmarks file. She checks this group periodically as her work proceeds.

Once you have an idea for a topic, you can post your own message to get feedback about your ideas. Remember, when posting to listservs and newsgroups, take care to compose a posting that shows you've put some serious thought into the topic. The message: "I am writing a paper on *Hamlet*, can anyone help me?" will probably only get sarcastic responses if it gets any responses at all. A carefully composed request that perks the interest of others in the group is much more likely to generate useful and interesting responses. While group members will very likely pass by a subject line like "Hamlet Paper," they'd probably be intrigued by a heading like "Is Ophelia a Manic Depressive?"

Step 5: Follow up on links uncovered in steps 2–4

Don't forget to keep notes on the sites you visit while you're narrowing and refining your topic; you never know

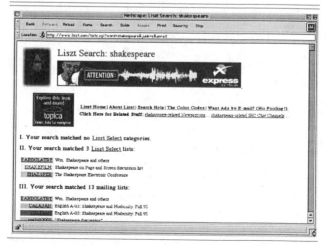

Figure 11.2: Results of a Liszt search for "shakespeare"

when they might become useful. After Cindy decided to focus here paper on Hamlet's madness, she looked back on her notes and revisited the Was Hamlet Mad? site at *http://www.hamlet.edmonton.ab.ca/WASHEMAD.HTM.*

Step 6: Gather additional material and conduct searches using Web search engines

Once you've done some preliminary research, it's time to dig deeper into your topic. The best way to find highly specialized information on the Web is using Web search engines (see page 32). Cindy decides to use AltaVista at *http://www.altavista.com/* to perform a phrase search for "William Shakespeare." By placing the name in quotation marks, she limits her search to sites which include the two names together. This search yields over 45,000 hits. She decides to focus on the play *Hamlet* using the + operator:

```
+"william shakespeare" +hamlet
```

This yields over 6,000 hits—greatly reduced, but still obviously too much information. She notices that her results contain a lot of film advertisements and festival notices. She modifies her search again to include madness and exclude films and festivals:

```
+madness +hamlet +shakespeare -film -festival
+ophelia
```

Now Cindy begins to feel as if her results are manageable. This search returns about 1,600 hits and she can tell that many of them specifically address the topic of Hamlet's madness.

Hamlet Navigator
http://www.clicknotes.com/pweller/Hamnavl/Madness.html
This is an entire site devoted to the subject of Hamlet's madness and includes references made by characters throughout the play that relate to whether or not Hamlet was mad.

Discussion of Hamlet: Madness
http://www-tech.mit.edu/Shakespeare/cgi-bin/commentary/get/Tragedy/hamlet/344.html
Here, Cindy finds a group discussing the madness of Hamlet and Ophelia. She realizes that mostly this is simply a forum

for the exchange of opinions, but it is a good place to generate ideas so she subscribes to be added to the discussion via
email.

Surfing with the Bard
http://www.ulen.com/shakespeare/
Cindy saves this URL because it has a link to Hamlet and a
lot of other Shakespeare links.

Cindy bookmarks all these URLs and other information
needed for documenting these sources in a text file. She saves
the entire text of the Hamlet Navigator page.

Step 7: Evaluate your sources

This step is actually ongoing. When Cindy looked at the
discussion page that debated Hamlet's madness and determined that most of the information was opinion, she was
evaluating the source. This is particularly important when
doing research on the Internet, where anyone can post or present information on any subject. It is not monitored or regu-
lated for authenticity by anyone except whoever's viewing it.
   More information on evaluating Internet sources can be
found in Chapter 1.

Step 8: Look for electronic texts
of works on the Web

While most copyrighted books and journals are not
freely available on the Web, famous works whose copyrights
have expired can be found in abundance. In the United
States, all copyrights for works published more than seventy-
five years ago have expired, so if you're writing about a work
over seventy-five years old, you may very likely find the
complete text on the Web. In Great Britain, copyrights expire fifty years after the death of the author, so you may even
find some works less than seventy-five years old on the Web
(for example, many works of D. H. Lawrence can be found
at the Bibliomania Web site, *http://www.bibliomania.com/
Fiction/dhl/*).
   Cindy found that the complete works of Shakespeare are
readily available on the Web, and some are even searchable.

For example, you could search *Hamlet* on The Complete Plays of William Shakespeare at ***http://www.ke.com.au/cgi -bin/texhtml?form=Shake***. Her search for *madness* found twenty-two instances of this word (see Figure 11.3). She could click on the word in the sample to be sent to the scene where the word was found.

It is important to look for alternate spellings or synonyms as well. Cindy searched for several: *Mad* returned twenty-one instances, *sick* had four, and there were none for *crazy* and *dementia*. If the work you are using does not have its own searchable database, you can conduct your own search of the text by using the "Find" command of your browser.

While counting instances of key words does not substitute for a close analysis of the text itself, searching Web text can alert you to key passages you may not have noticed otherwise. Some Web search engines even allow commands like "before" and "close to" which can further limit your search. Below are several sites which offer searchable text of literary works.

IPL Online Texts Collection
http://www.ipl.org/reading/books/

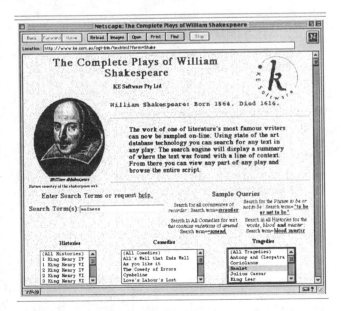

Figure 11.3: Searching for *madness* on The Complete Plays of William Shakespeare site

Electronic Text Center—University of Virginia
http://etext.lib.virginia.edu/english.html

The On-Line Books Page
http://www.cs.cmu.edu/books.html

Selected Poetry of Robert Browning (1812–1889)
*http://library.utoronto.ca/www/utel/rp/authors/browning
.html*

The Internet Classics Archive
http://classics.mit.edu/

Geoffrey Chaucer (ca.1343–1400)
http://www.luminarium.org/medlit/chaucer.htm

GEOFFREY CHAUCER ca. 1343–1400
*http://federalist.com/poetry/GEOFFREYCHAUCERcahall/
wwwboard.html*

IPL William Shakespeare's Complete Works
http://www.ipl.org/reading/shakespeare/shakespeare.html

Edmund Spenser Home Page
http://darkwing.uoregon.edu/~rbear/

Isle of Lesbos: Lesbian Poetry
http://www.sappho.com/poetry/

The Academy of American Poets
http://www.poets.org/

Step 9: Search for additional sources in the library

For most research projects, you should always supple-
ment the information you find on the Internet with resources from the traditional libraries. However, you can still
use the Internet to search the online catalog of your school
library and other libraries for books. Most online library catalogs are similar to each other, but it is helpful to read the
search directions for each one to ensure that you are getting
the best responses. An easy way to search many different libraries is using the Library of Congress WWW/Z39.50
Gateway at *http://lcweb.loc.gov/z3950/gateway.html#other*.
You can also search indexes, such as Carl UnCover
(*http://www.carl.org/*). This particular index provides access
to journal articles, which they can fax to you for a fee.

Step 10: Write your paper

Once you've collected enough information, it's time to begin composing. Cindy starts by going through the information she's collected and writing a thesis and an outline. As she began composing her paper, occasionally she had trouble motivating herself to write. Once again, the Web can help. Many sites are dedicated to student writing; here are some of the best:

The Online Writery
http://www.missouri.edu/~writery/

Purdue Online Writing Lab: Online Writing Lab
http://owl.english.purdue.edu/introduction.html

University of Texas Undergraduate Writing Center
http://uwc.fac.utexas.edu/resource/

Paradigm Online Writing Assistant
http://www.powa.org/

As Cindy writes, she is careful to document all sources she uses according to COS–Humanities style. For more on COS Style, see Chapter 10.

Additional sites for researching literature on the Web

Author sites

The Shakespeare Mystery
http://www2.pbs.org/wgbh/pages/frontline/shakespeare/

The Author Guru's List of Author Addresses
http://www.geocities.com/Athens/Acropolis/4617/authormail.html

Playwrights on the Web: International Playwrights & Their Online Plays
http://www.stageplays.com/writers.htm

An Index of Poets in Representative Poetry On-line
http://library.utoronto.ca/www/utel/rp/indexauthors.html

Criticism on the Web

Elizabethan Review
http://www.elizreview.com/

Ophelia
http://www.stg.brown.edu/projects/hypertext/landow/victorian/gender/ophelia.html

Sewanee Review
http://cloud9.sewanee.edu/sreview/Home.html

Hypermedia Joyce Studies
http://astro.temple.edu/~callahan/hjs/hjs.html

MFS
http://www.sla.purdue.edu/academic/engl/mfs/#ABOUT

Bakhtin on-line elsewhere
http://hippo.shef.ac.uk/uni/academic/A-C/bakh/online.html

Postmodernism, deconstructionism, criticism, and literary theory campfire messsage board
http://killdevilhill.com/postmodernchat/wwwboard.html

Voice of the Shuttle: Literary Theory Page
http://humanitas.ucsb.edu/shuttle/theory.html

Poetry Daily, a new poem every day
http://www.poems.com/~poems/home.htm

LitLinks
http://www.ualberta.ca/~amactavi/litlinks.htm

Zuzu's Petals Literary Links: General Reference Tools
http://www.zuzu.com/

VoS English Literature: English Literature Page
http://humanitas.ucsb.edu/shuttle/english.html

Directory of URLs Referenced in the Text

Search Engines

AltaVista
http://www.altavista.com

Ask Jeeves
http://www.askjeeves.com/

Excite
http://excite.com/

HotBot
http://www.hotbot.com/

Infoseek
http://infoseek.go.com/

Liszt Directory of Mailing Lists
http://www.liszt.com/

Lycos
http://www.lycos.com/

Mamma
http://www.mamma.com/

Savvy Search
http://savvysearch.com/

WebCrawler
http://webcrawler.com/

Subject Directories

The Argus Clearinghouse
http://www.clearinghouse.net/

The Internet Public Library
http://www.ipl.org/

WWW Virtual Library
http://www.vlib.org

Yahoo!
http://www.yahoo.com/

General research sites

Boolean Search Tutorial
http://www.learnthenet.com/ english/html/77advanc.htm

Carl UnCover
http://www.carl.org/

COS Web site
http://www.columbia.edu/cu/ cup/cgos/

Encarta
http://encarta.msn.com/

Encyclopedia Britannica
http://www.eb.com/

Grolier
http://www.grolier.com/

Library of Congress World Wide Web Home Page
http://lcWeb.loc.gov/

127

Library of Congress
WWW/Z39.50 Gateway
http://lcweb.loc.gov/z3950/
gateway.html#other

Using Cybersources Web site
http://www.devry-phx.edu/
lrnresrc/dowsc/integrty.htm

News sites
ABC
http://www.abcnews.com/

CNN
http://cnn.com/

MSNBC
http://msnbc.com/

New York Times
http://www.nytimes.com/

Seattle Times
http://www.seattletimes.com/

Time Magazine
http://pathfinder.com/time/

Washington Post
http://www.washingtonpost
.com/

Helper applications
Directory of plug-ins compatible with Netscape Navigator
http://www.netscape.com/
plugins/

RealAudio site
http://www.real.com/products/
player/

Stuffit
http:// www.aladdinsys.com/

WinZip
http://www.winzip.com

Technical help sites
The Art of Web Site Promotion
http://www.deadlock.com/
promote/

Creating Killer Web Sites
http://www.killersites.com/
tutorial/index.html

Forms
http://www.yahoo.com/
Computers_and_Internet/
Internet/World_Wide_Web/
Programming/Forms/

HTML commands
Introduction to HTML and
URLs site
http://www.utoronto.ca/
webdocs/HTMLdocs/
NewHTML/intro.html

Imagemap tutorial
http://www.webcom.com/
html/tutor/imagemaps.shtml

Netscape table tutorial
http://www.netscape.com/assist/
net_sites/table_assist.html

Server-side operations of the
Web
http://Web66.coled
.umn.edu/Cookbook/

Web-safe colors
http://www.lightsphere.com/
colors/

Authors on the Internet
The Author Guru's List of
Author Addresses
http://www.geocities.com/
Athens/Acropolis/4617/
authormail.html

D. H. Lawrence at the
Bibliomania Web site
http://www.bibliomania.com/
Fiction/dhl/

Discussion of Hamlet:
Madness
http://www-tech.mit.edu/
Shakespeare/cgi-bin/
commentary/get/Tragedy/
hamlet/344.html

Hamlet Navigator
*http://www.clicknotes.com/
pweller/Hamnavl/Madness
.html*

An Index of Poets in
Representative Poetry On-line
*http://library.utoronto.ca/
www/utel/rp/indexauthors
.html*

Playwrights on the Web:
International Playwrights &
Their Online Plays
*http://www.stageplays.com/
writers.htm*

Shakespeare newsgroup
*humanities.lit.authors
.shakespeare*

The Shakespeare Mystery
*http://www2.pbs.org/wgbh/
pages/frontline/shakespeare/*

Surfing with the Bard
*http://www.ulen.com/
shakespeare/*

Was Hamlet Mad?
*http://www.hamlet.edmonton
.ab.ca/WASHEMAD.HTM*

Online text collections

The Academy of American
Poets
http://www.poets.org/

The Complete Plays of
William Shakespeare
*http://www.ke.com.au/
cgibin/texhtml?form=Shake*

Edmund Spenser Home Page
*http://darkwing.uoregon
.edu/~rbear/*

Electronic Text Center—
University of Virginia
*http://etext.lib.virginia.edu/
english.html*

Geoffrey Chaucer
(ca.1343–1400)
*http://www.luminarium.org/
medlit/chaucer.htm*

GEOFFREY CHAUCER ca.
1343–1400
*http://federalist.com/poetry/
GEOFFREYCHAUCERcahall/
wwwboard.html*

The Internet Classics Archive
http://classics.mit.edu/

IPL Online Texts Collection
*http://www.ipl.org/reading/
books/*

Isle of Lesbos: Lesbian Poetry
http://www.sappho.com/poetry/

The On-Line Books Page
*http://www.cs.cmu.edu/books
.html*

Poetry Daily, a new poem
every day
*http://www.poems.com/~poems/
home.htm*

Selected Poetry of Robert
Browning (1812–1889)
*http://library.utoronto.ca/
www/utel/rp/authors/
browning.html*

Writing

The Online Writery
*http://www.missouri.edu/
~writery/*

Paradigm Online Writing
Assistant
http://www.powa.org/

Purdue Online Writing Lab:
Online Writing Lab
*http://owl.english.purdue.edu/
introduction.html*

University of Texas
Undergraduate Writing Center
*http://uwc.fac.utexas.edu/
resource/*

Literary criticism

Bakhtin on-line elsewhere
*http://hippo.shef.ac.uk/uni/
academic/A-C/bakh/online
.html*

Elizabethan Review
http://www.elizreview.com/

Hypermedia Joyce Studies
*http://astro.temple.edu/
~callahan/hjs/hjs.html*

LitLinks
*http://www.ualberta.ca/
~amactavi/litlinks.htm*

MFS
*http://www.sla.purdue.edu/
academic/engl/mfs/#ABOUT*

Ophelia
*http://www.stg.brown.edu/
projects/hypertext/landow/
victorian/gender/ophelia.html*

Postmodernism, deconstructionism, criticism, and literary
theory campfire messsage
board
*http://killdevilhill.com/
postmodernchat/wwwboard
.html*

Sewanee Review
*http://cloud9.sewanee.edu/
sreview/Home.html*

Voice of the Shuttle: Literary
Theory Page
*http://humanitas.ucsb.edu/
shuttle/theory.html*

VoS English Literature: English
Literature Page
*http://humanitas.ucsb.edu/
shuttle/english.html*

Zuzu's Petals Literary Links:
General Reference Tools
http://www.zuzu.com/

Miscellaneous

Diversity University MOO
moo.du.org 8888

J. D. Rockefeller
*http://voteview.gsia.cmu.edu/
entrejdr.htm*

Joke awards
*http://www.thecorporation
.com/icon/icon.html*

Microsoft's Department of
Justice Timeline:
*http://www.microsoft.com/
presspass/doj/timeline.htm*

Milos Forman interview page
*http://www.hollywood.com/
movietalk/celebrities/mforman/
html/sound.html*

Glossary

@ (the "at" sign) Used to separate the mailbox name from the domain name in e-mail addresses.

absolute URL The complete URL; used to refer to URLs outside of the current domain.

address Specialized URL for sending e-mail, consisting of a mailbox name and the domain name, separated by the @ sign. Also used to refer to any URL.

anchor The beginning point for a hypertext link. Anchors usually use underlined text (hot text) or images to indicate links.

angle bracket (>) 1. Used to denote a reply quotation in e-mail messages. 2. Used in pairs to surround HTML tags.

application Any type of commercial, shareware, or freeware computer program (usually with a user interface).

Archie A protocol which allows keyword searches of the contents of FTP sites (primarily for names of freeware and shareware applications and graphic files).

ASCII text (pron. *askey*) Also known as "text only" format, the basic, unformatted numbers, letters, and symbols supported by most computer operating systems.

asynchronous Communication or other interaction that takes place with a substantial delay, e.g., e-mail, answering machines.

attribute (HTML) A modification to an HTML tag which gives information about how it is to be applied.

131

AU An audio file format commonly found on the World Wide Web.

authoring The process of creating hypermedia content for the World Wide Web.

bit The smallest unit of computer memory. Can have only two values, 1 or 0.

bookmark An electronic pointer to a Gopher, FTP, or Web site that can be recalled for future reference. A list of bookmarks is known as "favorites" or a "hotlist."

Boolean Logical search operators that allow a user to refine the scope of keyword searches. The simple Boolean operators are *and*, *or*, and *not*.

bots (robots) Objects in MOO environments which are programmed to interact with readers.

browser A client which allows users to view pages on the World Wide Web. The two most popular browsers are Microsoft Internet Explorer and Netscape Navigator.

browsing The process of viewing Web pages with a browser.

byte A unit of computer memory corresponding to eight bits. A byte contains enough information to specify one character.

CD-ROM A compact disc used for storing computer files. Many new formats have been introduced recently, including CD-RW, DVD, and CD-R.

channel Also referred to as a "line." An IRC channel is roughly equivalent to a CB radio frequency. Users join a channel to participate in the discussion that takes place among people logged on to that frequency.

chat 1. A somewhat derogatory term used to describe newsgroups or listservs that are geared toward the discussion of nonacademic topics. 2. A term often heard when talking about Internet Relay Chat (IRC). The IRC channels are often called "chat lines" and the conversations that take place on these channels are often referred to as "chat."

Clarinet Newsfeeds from Reuters and the Associated Press in the form of Usenet newsgroups. Institutions must pay a fee in order to subscribe to groups provided by the Clarinet company.

client Software which communicates with a server to provide an easier interface for a user.

Columbia Online Style A method of documenting online sources for academic research, usually in conjunction with MLA or APA style.

Common Gateway Interface (CGI) A program which resides on a server and handles complex information requests. CGIs act as mediators between a source of information on a server and a client. They are most commonly used to process forms in HTML.

compression Manipulation of a file to decrease the amount of memory it consumes. Compression can be either "lossy," meaning some information is lost in compression, or "lossless," meaning all information is retained.

directory A subdivision in a computer file system (known as a "folder" in some operating systems). Directories can contain files, applications, or other directories.

directory path The complete set of nested directories needed to locate a particular file. In URLs, each directory name is separated by a slash.

discussion list See *listserv.*

domain An element of an Internet or e-mail address specified by an organization or sub-organization on the Internet (e.g., *netscape.com,* or *utexas.edu*).

DOS See *operating system.*

downloading Retrieving a file or application from a remote host over the Internet.

element (HTML) Instructions within an HTML document, along with the text to which they apply. For example, the boldface text element, `<B> this text will be bold </B>`.

e-mail (electronic mail) A form of Internet communication used to send all types of electronic correspondence to individuals or groups of Internet-connected users around the world.

e-mail address See *address.*

emote To virtually represent an action during the real-time conversations on IRCs and MOOs. For example, a user named Socrates could type `:listens intently`, and

the text transmitted to other participants would read
Socrates listens intently.

emoticons Pictures made of text symbols attempting to express emotions in e-mail messages, newsgroup postings,
and real-time discussions. The basic Internet emoticon is
the "smiley," a sideways happy face: :-) (turn your head
to the left to see it).

FAQ (Frequently Asked Questions) A document which collects and responds to some of the most common questions about a particular aspect of the Internet or about a
particular topic, especially newsgroups and listservs.

favorites See *bookmark*.

file An electronic document. Files can be in ASCII text, in
a format for a particular program, or in a standardized
format for sound, graphics, or video (e.g., WAV, GIF, or
MPEG).

file name The name of a file, including any extensions such
as *.html* or *.gif*, but not including its directory path.

flame A message or posting attacking a message or an individual. A flame usually has a confrontational tone and
offers little or no constructive criticism.

form (HTML) Mechanism which allows Web site visitors
to send information back to a server.

freeware Software distributed free of charge.

FTP (File Transfer Protocol) An early, but still frequently
used system of downloading and uploading files on the
Internet.

fuzzy search A search for any occurrence of a sequence of characters, regardless of whether they form an entire word.

GIF (Graphical Interchange Format) (pron. *jiff*) A compressed graphics file format frequently used for images
on the World Wide Web. GIF files save memory by limiting the number of colors in an image.

GIF 89a See *GIF*.

Gopher A system of Internet protocols and directory
structures that allows users to connect to remote hosts,
access directories of information, and download files.
In addition, Gopher sites can be searched for directory
names, file titles, or text contained in individual files.

Gopher server A centralized server that offers hierarchically organized information to a user via a Gopher client. Also called Gopherhost.

Gopherspace The realm of the Internet dedicated to Gopher. A good place to find archaic computer programming jokes.

hardware The mechanical portion of a computer system.

helper application Software that works with an Internet application (such as a browser) to add additional features (such as the capability to listen to real-time audio).

hit 1. An item returned from a keyword search. 2. A single visit to a Web site.

home page Conventional name given to a central site on the World Wide Web. This name can be used both for the central page of an organization site and for the personal page of an individual within an organization.

host 1. An Internet-connected machine which serves files to various clients. 2. Any Internet-connected machine.

hotlist See *bookmark*.

hot text Text in a hypertext document which is linked to another document. The most common way of linking documents on the Web. Hot text is generally colored and underlined to indicate that clicking on it will take the user to another document.

HTML (Hypertext Markup Language) A scripting language used to turn plain text and other elements (such as images) into the integrated pages we see on the Web.

HTTP (Hypertext Transport Protocol) An Internet protocol which allows for the transfer of hypertext files from a Web server to a Web client application.

hypermedia A medium which extends the principles of hypertext to document types other than text.

hypertext A text authoring medium with no predetermined organizational structure which allows authors to freely link any portion of a document with any other portion, or with other documents.

image editor An application which allows users to create and edit image files.

imagemap An image which has been "mapped" by HTML

commands so that clicking on different portions of it will link the user to different sites or files.

inline image   An image which has been inserted into the design of a Web page.

interface   The features of an application which mediate a user's interaction with the program. Generally speaking, the more intuitive the interface is to a user, the easier it will be to run the program.

Internet   The worldwide network of computers that allows distribution of e-mail, browsing the Web, and countless other ways to access and distribute information.

IP address (Internet Protocol Address)   The address which is specific to a single computer and identifies it for the purpose of interacting with other computers on the Internet.

IRC (Internet Relay Chat)   A system of Internet protocols and programs which allows users to participate on topic-centered, real-time discussion channels.

ISP (Internet Service Provider)   A service which allows individual users to connect to the Internet via phone or cable TV lines.

Java   A programming language which allows computers running on different operating systems to run the same programs. Java functions, typically used for graphics, animation, or complex data management tasks, are actually performed by applications ("applets") which reside on servers rather than individual PCs.

JPEG (Joint Photographic Experts Group)   (pron. *JAY-peg*) A graphics file format frequently used for images on the World Wide Web. JPEG files are typically most effective for photographs and offer several different levels of compression, with higher compression resulting in more loss of file resolution.

keyword   A word or group of words intended to express the subject of a document. Used by Web search engines to list relevant resources.

kilobyte (K)   A unit of computer memory corresponding to 1,024 bytes.

link   A hypertext connection between documents, sites, and other media. Note that *link* is commonly used both as a noun to indicate the actual connection between one node and another, and as a verb to indicate the process by which this connection is achieved.

Listproc A type of mailing list software. See also *listserv*.

listserv Also known as a "mailing list" or "list." A program which allows mail to be sent to a group of addresses at once.

literal search A search for an exact phrase or grouping of words, usually indicated with quotation marks.

local In the same directory as the current file. In HTML coding, local files can be accessed using relative URLs.

lurk To read a newsgroup or e-mail list for a period of time without posting messages.

Macintosh See *operating system*. See also *platform*.

mailbox name The specific identification or name given to an e-mail user. In conjunction with the domain name, it makes up the e-mail address using the syntax `mailboxname@domainname`.

mailreader Also known as a "mail client." A program which provides an easy interface for reading, composing, posting, and downloading e-mail messages.

mail server A server which organizes, stores, and distributes e-mail messages to various users.

Majordomo A type of mailing list software. See also *listserv*.

modem Short for "modulater-demodulater," a device used to connect computers via a telephone line or other communication link to a server. When you connect to the Internet at school your workstation may be directly wired to a server, but if you connect at home you will most likely need to use a modem.

moderator Person responsible for determining the relevancy of messages posted to a moderated newsgroup or listserv. A moderator forwards only "appropriate" messages to the group.

MOV/MOOV A video format often used on the World Wide Web.

MPEG (pron. *empeg*) A video format often used on the World Wide Web.

MU*s (also MUSHs, Tiny MUSHs, MOOs, etc.) Text-based virtual spaces ("Multi User Dungeons" or "Domains") which allow users to interact in real time with other users or with the textual environment. The different acronyms refer to different programs which perform similar functions.

name search A search for the first and last name of a person. Usually indicated by capitalizing both terms.

netiquette A set of rules for behavior on the Internet, usually dictated by convenience and common sense.

newsfeed A message posted to a newsgroup which originates from a wire service or other traditional news source.

newsgroups Topic-centered sites where visitors can exchange articles, messages, or other media. See also *Usenet*.

newsreader A news client.

news server Also known as a news host. A server which organizes, stores, and distributes newsgroup messages.

nickname 1. An address book entry for one or more e-mail addresses. When a user types the nickname, the computer sends that message to each of the addresses in the nickname file. 2. A character name used to log on to IRC channels.

node A hypertext site which organizes multiple links. Nodes can contain any combination of text, links, graphics, sound, and video.

operating system The software which controls the basic operations of the computer. Examples include MacOS, DOS, and Unix. These systems are generally incompatible with each other.

page Part of a Web site corresponding to a single HTML file.

PC 1. Also referred to as "IBM compatible," indicates a computer which runs the DOS operating system (usually with the graphical user interface Windows). 2. Used less often to indicate any personal computer.

Photo CD A type of CD-ROM containing photo images. Also used to refer to the format Photo CD images are saved in.

phrase search See *literal search*.

pixel A single dot, or element, of a picture. Image sizes on the Web are measured in pixels.

plagiarism Intentionally or accidentally presenting someone else's work as one's own. A serious offense—can be grounds for failing a course or expulsion.

platform A computer with a given type of operating system, for example, Macintosh, PC, or Unix.

plug-in See *helper application.*

post 1. To send an electronic message to an e-mail discussion list or newsgroup. Also used as a noun to refer to the message itself.   2. To upload a Web site to a Web server.

protocol The "language" that a client and server use to distinguish various types of Internet media.

readme file Gives information about a piece of software or an Internet forum. Titling a file "readme" almost assures that it will never be read.

real time Communication or other interaction that occurs almost instantaneously, as in IRCs and MOOs, allowing users to communicate in a way which resembles face-to-face conversation. Contrast to e-mail and newsgroup messages, which are asynchronous.

relative URL A partial URL used to specify locations within the current domain.

reply quotation A copy of a message which is included in the reply to the message. Most mail clients and newsreaders place angle brackets (>) in front of a quotation in order to distinguish it from a new message.

robot search engine A search engine which automatically visits Web sites or other Internet sites and catalogs them based on a predetermined set of criteria.

scanner A machine which converts photographs and other physical images into electronic files.

search engine A program usually accessed via a Web site that allows users to perform keyword searches on the Internet (e.g., AltaVista, Infoseek).

search index A directory of services on the Internet organized hierarchically.

server 1. Software that provides information to client programs. Clients and servers "talk" to each other to allow the transfer of files and protocols across the Internet. 2. The machine on which a server program is located.

shareware Like *freeware*, software which is made available through the Internet. The authors of shareware ask for a small voluntary fee from users.

shell A program that interprets commands typed at a terminal.

signature file Pre-formatted text attached to the bottom of most e-mail and newsgroup messages which generally contains the author's name, e-mail address, and institutional affiliation (if any). Signature files can also contain carefully constructed ASCII text pictures and favorite quotations.

site A collection of documents on the Internet providing a single set information to users who access the location.

slide show A series of textual screens that scroll by to deliver information in a MOO.

smiley See *emoticon*.

software A computer program written to perform various tasks, as opposed to *hardware*, which refers to the mechanical parts of a computer system. See also *application*.

source document The underlying HTML document that produces a Web page when viewed with a Web browser. Most Web browsers allow a user to "view" the source document of any page found on the Web.

spam 1. E-mail sent to large numbers of recipients without their first requesting it. 2. Postings of irrelevant messages to newsgroups or listservs. 3. Any attempt to push unwanted information on Internet users by making use of repetitious computing power. 4. (Rarely used) (*cap.*) A pork-based luncheon meat.

subject directory See *search index*.

surfing The process of navigating from site to site on the Internet (usually the Web) in a nonlinear and non-hierarchical manner.

tags (HTML) Commands in HTML documents contained in angle brackets. Tags usually work in pairs, with a closing tag dictating where the effect of the tag ends.

targeting Connecting directly to a Web site or Gopherhost by entering a known address.

Telnet A terminal emulation protocol. With a Telnet client application, such as NCSA Telnet, you can establish a connection to a remote computer.

text only See *ASCII text*.

thread A newsgroup or listserv posting and a series of re-plies on the same topic, usually with the same subject heading.

tunneling Accessing a site (usually a Gopher site) by digging down through various directories or subdirectories.

Unix See *operating system*. See also *platform*.

uploading Placing a file or application on a remote host over the Internet. Often used to put text, sound, graphics, video, and HTML files on a Web server for publication.

URL (Uniform Resource Locator) The address assigned to each document on the Internet. Consists of the protocol, followed by two slashes, the domain name and type, the directory path, and the file name.

Usenet Part of the Internet which facilitates the exchange of messages and discussion. The broad classification of Usenet contains thousands of topic-centered newsgroups organized hierarchically by name.

user name or **user's name** See *mailbox name*.

Veronica A search engine which can locate items on most of the Internet's Gopher servers using keywords and Boolean operators.

WAIS (Wide Area Information Search) A search engine configured to locate and retrieve information from a designated set of documents. Unlike Veronica or the Web search engines, WAIS performs local rather than general Internet searches.

WAV An audio file format.

Web authoring system Software that allows users to create Web pages without using the HTML language.

Web browser See *browser*.

Web-safe colors A set of 216 colors for Web pages which display accurately on all properly equipped platforms.

window A framed area on a computer screen that allows the user to view information without affecting the rest of the screen.

Windows See *operating system.*

workstation An individual computer usually connected to a network but primarily occupied by a single user. Used throughout this book to designate a personal computer where a user can operate local client software.

World Wide Web Abbreviated *WWW* or *the Web.* A worldwide system for distributing hypermedia, allowing users to easily navigate between sites and post their own documents.

For more information about computer terms, visit the Free On-Line Dictionary of Computing at *http://www.instantweb.com/~foldoc/.*

Index

143